Barbies and Battlescars

Facing Your Demons, Embracing Your Inner Schizo, and Finding Purpose One F*ckity F*ck at a Time

By Jessica Rose

Published by The Jessica Rose Experience
ISBN: 979-8-9977678-0-8

INTRODUCTION

Well, here we are. You picked up this book—maybe out of curiosity, maybe out of desperation, maybe because someone shoved it in your hands and said, "Trust me, you need this." Whatever the reason, I need you to know something right up front: you're not about to read a fairy tale, a neatly tied-up self-help manual, or some "Ten Steps to Perfect Happiness" crap that looks good on Instagram but doesn't work worth a damn in real life. What you're about to read is a story—a messy, painful, hilarious, terrifying, hopeful story—of what it looks like to walk through hell and somehow come out the other side, not just alive, but still fighting.

This book is not written from a mountaintop with a halo glowing over my head. It's written from the trenches, from the aftershocks, from the scars that still sometimes ache when the weather changes. It's written by someone who has been through trauma that could have swallowed me whole, and who found ways—sometimes clumsy, sometimes brilliant, often absurd—to keep going anyway. You're going to get the good, the bad, and the laugh-so-hard-you-snort parts of a life that never fit neatly into a box. If you've ever looked at your life and thought, *"Well, fuck. What now?"* then congratulations—you're in the right place. That question is basically the soundtrack of my existence.

Every time I thought I had something figured out, life threw another curveball: a fractured childhood, an unstable home, moving across continents like some diplomatic ping-pong ball, the gut punch of mental illness, the devastating weight of addiction tearing through my family, abusive relationships, and my own desperate battles with suicidal thoughts and attempts. And yet, alongside the chaos, there were also absurd adventures, stolen moments of joy, wild nights, fierce friendships, and an inner drive to not just survive but eventually thrive.

This isn't a sob story. I'm not here to make you feel sorry for me. I'm here to tell the truth—the kind of truth we usually shove in the back of a closet and hope no one sees. I'm here to drag the skeletons out, dress them in Barbie outfits, and let them dance on the table while we pour another drink. Because that's how you strip the shame away. You own it. You laugh at it. You tell it out loud before it eats you alive.

Let's be clear about what you're in for. This isn't a step-by-step guide to living your best life. You're not going to find "The Secret" here. There's no manifestation chart at the end, no workbook to fill out in pastel markers. If that's what you came for, I promise you'll be disappointed.

What you will find are stories—real, unpolished, often messy stories about what it's like to grow up in a family fractured by illness and addiction, to move between cultures and identities until you don't know which version of yourself is the real one, to live with depression that feels like a weighted blanket made of lead, to attempt to disappear more than once, and to claw your way back into life again and again. You'll find humor—the inappropriate kind that keeps you alive when everything else feels unbearable. You'll find raw honesty, because sugarcoating has never helped anyone survive. And, if I've done my job right, you'll find pieces of yourself in these pages, even if your story looks completely different on the surface.

This isn't a book about being broken. It's a book about being human. And being human, as it turns out, is fucking hard. Here's the thing about trauma: it either hardens you or it gives you the sharpest, darkest sense of humor on the planet. Sometimes both. For me, humor was oxygen. It was the only way I could breathe through the moments that should have suffocated me. When I talk about Barbie personas or about releasing ducklings into a swimming pool like some deranged Disney princess, I'm not making light of the pain. I'm showing you the absurdity that lives alongside the pain. Because the truth is, you can't survive trauma without learning to laugh at the ridiculousness of it all. And if you can laugh—even when you're crying—you can keep going.

That's why this book isn't written in hushed tones with solemn background music. It's loud, messy, often funny, and sometimes shocking. Just like life.

If you've ever felt fractured—like you're playing different versions of yourself depending on the room you're in—this book is for you. If you've ever wondered if the things you do to cope make you "crazy," this book is for you. If you've ever thought you were too broken, too messy, too complicated to be worth loving, this book is definitely for you.

This book is also for anyone who loves someone who has walked through trauma, addiction, or mental illness. Because sometimes the only way to understand what's happening in someone else's head is to hear it spoken out loud in all its messy glory.

And if you're someone who just loves a good, wild, true story told without filters—well, buckle up. You're going to get more than your money's worth.

Each chapter dives into different seasons of my life, from the wild diplomat's-kid adventures of my childhood to the fractured teenage years, from the Barbie personas I created to survive young adulthood to the abusive relationships I had to claw my way out of. You'll see the chaos, the humor, the pain, and the moments of healing. You'll see how identity fractures under pressure, and how it's possible to piece yourself back together again—maybe not perfectly, but strong in new ways.

Along the way, I'll share the lessons I've learned—not as a guru, but as someone who has had to learn them the hard way. Lessons about taking responsibility even when the fire is burning, about finding humor in the absurd, about the importance of therapy, about the necessity of chosen family, and about the fact that healing isn't a one-time finish line but a messy, ongoing process.

There will be times when it's heavy, because life is heavy. But there will also be times when you laugh so hard you forget what page you're on. Both are essential. Both are real. And both are what survival looks like.

I wrote this book because I got tired of pretending. Tired of walking into rooms with a smile while hiding scars under my sleeves. Tired of people only seeing the polished version and never knowing what it took to stand upright. I wrote this book because I know what it feels like to believe you're the only one carrying this kind of weight—and I want you to know you're not alone.

I also wrote it because I believe stories save lives. They saved mine. Every time I heard someone else speak the unspeakable, it cracked the door open for me to keep going. If my story can do that for you—even just for one person—then all the mess was worth something.

A Note Before We Begin

I want to be upfront: There are parts of this book that may be hard to read. I talk openly about abuse, addiction, suicide attempts, and trauma. If those are things that hit close to home for you, please take care of yourself. Read at your own pace. Skip sections if you need to. There's no prize for finishing it in one sitting. This is about connection, not endurance.

But I also want to promise you something: This book is not hopeless. It's not a dirge. It's not tragedy porn. It's about survival, resilience, and the absurdity of being alive when life has every reason to take you out. It's about the messy, complicated, hilarious, painful, beautiful business of being human.

So, what are you in for? You're in for the truth. You're in for stories that might make you cry, definitely make you laugh, and maybe, just maybe, make you feel less alone in your own chaos. You're in for a ride through a life that has been anything but ordinary, told with the kind of honesty that doesn't flinch from the ugly parts.

If you've ever thought you were too messy to matter, too fractured to be whole, too lost to be found—this book is here to call bullshit on that. You're not too far gone. None of us are.

So grab a drink, settle in, and get ready. Because life is messy, healing is messy, and this book is messy. But somewhere in the middle of all that mess, you're going to find pieces of yourself reflected back at you. And maybe, just maybe, you'll walk away knowing that if I can survive my shitshow of a life, then you can survive yours, too.

Welcome to the chaos. Let's dive in.

TABLE OF CONTENTS

Part 1:
It Was Fucking Traumatic

Well, F*ck. What Now?

Life has a way of knocking you on your ass and then politely asking if you'd like another round. And, if you're anything like me, the only response is a deep breath, a quick reality check, and the recurring question: *Well, f*ck. What now?* That's been the theme of my life—navigating impossible situations, reinventing myself in new countries, learning to survive when everything felt like it was collapsing, and even standing in front of a mirror wondering, *Does this muumuu make me look fat?*

This book is about all of it—the good, the bad, the laugh-so-you-don't-cry moments, and the absolute clusterf*cks of life that shape who we are. It's about surviving trauma, finding purpose, and, most importantly, doing it all with a sense of humor. Because if I didn't laugh, I'd probably still be curled up in the fetal position somewhere.

The Serengeti (or Was It Jurassic Park?)

My childhood was...let's say, *unconventional.* My dad was a diplomat, which meant we moved—a lot. My parents met in Iran when my dad was stationed at the consulate there, and my mother was visiting her parents who were in the military and were stationed there. Thank goodness for their adventurous spirits because the product of their happenstance meeting was me and a shitload of frequent flyer miles.

My mom went into labor and somehow made it to the safety of Fairfax, VA, for my debut into this crazy world, but it wasn't long before we were back in a foreign land, finding ourselves in Calcutta, India. I don't have a lot of early life memories from here, but from what I hear from my dad, I should probably be happy for that small blessing. By the time I was 5 I found myself in Zimbabwe. If that sounds glamorous, let me assure you—it was more *Indiana Jones meets National Geographic* than it was *princess in a palace.*

Case in point: The backyard of our house in Zimbabwe was, to my small self, basically the Serengeti. And by *Serengeti,* I mean it might as well have been *Jurassic Park*. If you're imagining rolling plains, majestic sunsets, and wildlife documentaries narrated by David Attenborough, you're only half right. Now, picture a feral little child scaling a 10-foot stone wall just to get a closer look at a zebra or something equally ridiculous. That was me.

I was drawn to animals like a Disney princess who took a wrong turn and ended up in a B-list survival movie. Our house was always full of critters—whether they were meant to be there or not. At one point, I convinced our nanny to bring home a crate of ducklings from the market, which I promptly released into the swimming pool. My parents came home to find our luxurious backyard oasis transformed into *Duck Lagoon*—a decision that, in hindsight, probably should have gotten me evicted from the household. Then there was the injured crow that crash-landed into our window and somehow became my pet. To me, this was normal life.

Life was fun—I've found pictures of my platinum-blonde self, decked out in a full saree with bells and bangles, and my father would reminisce about how he and my mom would prop me up on the table, letting me dance and jingle my little heart out for family, guests, and any poor suckers within eyesight.

Growing up overseas left its marks on me—some of it obvious, some of it delightfully confusing. One of these marks became painfully clear when we popped back to the US for a short stint in North Carolina while Dad did language training at Duke. The catch? I didn't exactly speak fluent *English*. Well, not in a way anyone Stateside would recognize. Having spent my early years in India and Zimbabwe, my linguistic skills were...let's call them "creatively curated." I spoke a glorious jumble of Hindi, Swahili, and something *vaguely* resembling English—a dialect so unique that only my brother could understand me. My dad loved to say I was the smartest kid he'd ever met…just tragically incapable of communicating with anyone outside our living room.

The Woman Who Raised Me (and Raised Hell)

My mother was a force of nature. She was vibrant, fierce, and had the kind of beauty that could make a room stop—but life had not been gentle to her. She had struggled with illness, loss, and the impossible task of trying to hold everything together while fighting battles no one else saw. The 1980s weren't exactly the golden age of mental health awareness. Back then, if a woman was struggling, society didn't say, *Hey, let's get her some help.* No, they just handed her a prescription and a pat on the head. My mother had hepatitis from a contaminated hospital during her pregnancy in Iran and was put on what can only be presumed as trial medications that did more harm than good. That, combined with addiction and untreated mental health issues, meant that by the time I was old enough to notice, our relationship had already started to fracture.

But here's the thing: My mother *loved* me. She loved my brother. She wanted to be everything we needed her to be, but life had dealt her one losing hand after another, and she played them the only way she knew how. And as a child, I didn't see the complexity—I just saw the fallout.

When Reality Sets In

Fast-forward to sixth grade. My parents had split when I was around 8 and while dad flew off to another distant land, my mother, half-brother and I moved to Florida. It was the first time I realized that my version of normal wasn't actually *normal.* As a kid, I had been obsessed with the sitcoms on *Nick at Nite*—staying up all night watching *The Donna Reed Show*, *My Three Sons*, *Bewitched*, and *Mr. Ed.* It's not like I truly expected life to be wrapped up neatly in a 30-minute episode, laugh track included, but I still found myself wishing for even a sliver of the security those families had. I caught glimpses of it at my friends' houses—the kind of stability that came with predictable dinners, parents who weren't juggling bills, and a general absence of social workers on speed dial. And the more I saw it, the more I realized just how much I *didn't* have it.

At home, my mom struggled to work due to illness. Strangers cycled in and out like our front door was a revolving audition room for "Questionable Life Choices: The Musical," and my brother's constant dalliances with drugs, breaking the law, and general teenage delinquency wasn't helping. I didn't fully understand what was happening, but I knew one thing for certain: Home was not where I wanted to be.

There were times when the food situation was lacking, and I'd dig through couch cushions for loose change just to have an excuse to walk to the corner store for a soda and a Slim Jim. More and more, I found myself at my best friend Anna's house. She slept over at my place *one* time, and that was apparently enough for her mom to decide, very gently, that future hangouts should probably happen at their house instead. Message received. Loud and clear.

Before long, I was at Anna's so much it felt like I lived there part-time, like some kind of unofficial, unspoken custody arrangement no one acknowledged. I don't think anyone at my house even noticed I was gone. At some stage, my dad had started to realize that something was not okay. About fucking time.

Escape to the Land of the Rising Sun

Next thing I knew, I was on a flight to Japan, where my dad was starting a new assignment. And while you'd think that would be the start of my *rescue story*, it's never that simple. I didn't actually want to be there. While life with mom was hard, I felt like I was abandoning her—like my dad was stealing me away and leaving her behind in a hellhole. She needed help, my brother needed help, and I was being ripped away. My anger and helplessness, fueled by preteen hormones, ignited a resentment towards my dad that impacted our relationship for the duration of my teen years. I was too young to understand the complexities that adults have to endure, with the constant barrage of responsibility, relationships, the profound impact of wrong choices, and, well, life.

After a while, things actually started to feel… normal-ish. I made friends, I liked our home. For a brief shining moment I thought, *Oh wow, look at me, thriving like a semi-feral child who's been socialized.*

Tokyo had been its own bubble-wrapped fantasy land. We lived in this super-sheltered compound full of military and embassy families—three giant towers plopped in the middle of Roppongi like a diplomatic Lego set. Inside the walls, everything was clean and safe and structured. Outside the walls, about a mile away, was Tokyo City: neon lights, arcades, skyscrapers, and enough chaos to make Times Square look like it needs a nap.

Thirteen-year-old me was too busy starring in her own personal daytime drama called "I'm Mad at My Dad: Season Infinity." I was livid. I blamed him for tearing apart our family, for every hardship, for my mother's slide into addiction, for the emotional weather patterns of the entire universe. If a butterfly sneezed in Brazil, somehow it was my dad's fault.

I was so laser-focused on the life I *should have had* that I completely ignored the fact that I was living a life many adults would sacrifice a kidney for. I wish I could go back and scream at teenage me, "HELLO? You are living in JAPAN. JAPAN. You're thirteen. Pull your head out of your hormonal storm cloud and look around!"

But nope. I was too busy rage-spiraling about all the wrong things, blind to the ridiculously cool things happening right in front of me.

I was able to recognize some of the good things, though. On the compound there were pools, koi gardens, and tennis courts, and we would often play Manhunt until midnight like it was our full time jobs. The Marine security guards (MSGs) lived on the compound, so we were ridiculously safe, which meant that we had this freedom and safety that I would never experience again.

Listen—you put a bunch of military and embassy brats together, and suddenly we're running around like tiny, unhinged special-ops recruits. We weren't doing cute little "Tag, you're it!" moments. Oh no. We were out there constructing actual booby traps, wearing full camouflage, climbing trees like caffeinated raccoons, and building rope courses that OSHA would have passed out over. We were the type of kids who would go to the rec center, start playing Risk at noon and not emerge for an entire presidential administration. We'd do 24-hour campouts, digging 5 foot holes, covering them with twigs and laughing like manic woodland goblins when someone fell in, like a darkly twisted preamble to *Mean Girls*.

Growing up, my dad always had strong opinions on religion—mainly that it was organized nonsense. He was an agnostic who loved to poke holes in religious doctrine, and like him, I didn't associate with any particular faith. But at the time, I was fascinated by Buddhism—the philosophy, the meditation, the whole idea of detachment from suffering. So it was almost comical that, in the midst of all this chaos, I found myself enrolled in a Catholic school—plaid kilt, button-up white shirt, and the looming presence of nuns and crucifixes everywhere I turned. The irony wasn't lost on me.

The nuns who ran the school were a no-nonsense squad of holy enforcers who had little patience for my Chatty Cathy tendencies during mass or rebellious antics, like when I once hijacked a school recital and swapped out our approved song for Madonna's "Like a Prayer." If you remember that music video, you already know this went over about as well as a thong at a Vatican brunch.

I didn't realize it at the time, but looking back, I was actually happy. I wish I could go back in time to visit my 13-year-old self, shake her, and say, "Let all the anger go! Look around! Soak up all the beauty and wonder! Go be a kid. You deserve it!" Although I'm pretty sure that little kid would have given me the middle finger.

Despite the incredible opportunity of living in Japan, I couldn't shake the guilt gnawing at me—knowing that life back home wasn't as kind to Nick or my mom. I was too stubborn, or maybe just too naïve, to see that this life with my dad could have set me on an entirely different path—one without the years of mental torment that would follow. Instead, I felt untethered. My dad was busy, I blamed him for my mom being ill, my home life felt hollow, and before I even realized it, depression had wrapped itself around me like a 100-pound weighted blanket I never asked for.

So, when my dad finally caved and sent me back to Florida, I convinced myself it was my chance to hit reset—to finally step into my own version of *The Donna Reed Show*. Spoiler alert: that's not exactly how it played out.

But wait! It gets worse.

When I got back to the States, my mom, my brother Nick, and I moved into a very nice house, two miles from the beach. My dad was sending money for my care, but I always wondered where that money went.

My mom was a shell of herself. That whole period is a blur, but I remember the emptiness, this heavy, suffocating quiet that settled over everything. Sometimes, she just wasn't there mentally. There was no hint of the vibrant woman she once was. She was drained. When she was home, she slept a lot. Other times, she wasn't there physically, either. Late nights turned into overnights. Overnights turned into days.

Nick was sinking deeper into addiction. He felt like a complete stranger to me. I was scared to be at home alone with him and the "friends" that squatted at our house and seemed to never leave. For some kids with less-than-stellar home lives, school becomes their saving grace, but for me, school was just another part of my prolonged pain and discomfort.

I didn't fit in at school. Anna, along with my other old friends, had somehow blossomed into girls off the pages from *Teen* magazine, and I hadn't caught up. I went from being a badass, Manhunt-playing diplomat's kid in Tokyo to a weird, awkward, thrift-store-clad misfit in Florida. It was like someone had taken my life, shaken it up in a snow globe, and then smashed it on the ground for good measure.

I felt utterly disconnected. By the time I returned, the world had moved on without me. My schoolmates, deeply rooted in American culture, navigated life with a familiarity I no longer shared. I'd left the safety of our compound only to find myself among preteens and teens who had never glimpsed the variety and experiences of the world beyond. It was jarring—and profoundly isolating.

Looking back on that part of my life, I should have gone full fucking feral and embraced being the weird kid. I should have rocked that shit, owned who I was, unapologetically. Yeah, I grew up all over the place. Yeah, my accent was basically a global sampler platter. Yeah, my personality was a chaotic mixtape of everywhere I'd ever lived, slapped together by a drunk assembly line that clearly did not follow the instructions.

But instead of letting all that shine through, I just tried to blend in, like I was folding myself into emotional origami. I was so desperate to feel "normal" that I sanded off every edge that made me interesting.

And when I think about that younger version of me, and all the kids out there bouncing from country to country in the foreign service or military, feeling like they're permanently the "other," I just want to grab them by the shoulders and say, "Stop chasing someone else's idea of perfection. Perfect doesn't exist. It never did."

At some point, my grandparents took me in, but no matter what, I always seemed to end up back with Mom and Nick. That stretch of my life is emotionally charged, tangled in a haze of memories I've mostly blocked out—some last-ditch effort at self-preservation. Even after 30 years and countless therapy sessions, it still feels like someone else's life, like a bad movie sequence I watched but never actually lived.

Things steadily progressed from shit show to full-blown, real-life train wreck. My brother wasn't my brother anymore; he was a stranger wearing his face. An imposter. The person I'd grown up with, the one who protected me, made me laugh, and kept the world from feeling so damn heavy, was gone.

I hated the version that replaced him. I hated what he'd become. He'd been my savior, my best friend, my safe person. But he killed that version of himself somewhere along the way, leaving me alone with the ghost of who he used to be.

While I was grieving the brother I'd lost, the rest of the house was collapsing right along with him. My mom started dating this guy, Eric, who was ten, maybe fifteen years younger than her, the kind of man who seems harmless enough until you realize "harmless" is his cover story. Mostly, he was a bad influence. They were drunk—or whatever else—a lot.

They'd stumble home and either pass out, fight, or both. Night after night, their screaming ricocheted through the house, shaking the walls. When Eric got drunk enough, the anger turned physical. I'd wake up to broken lamps, shattered frames, fresh holes punched into the drywall, like the house itself was trying to recoil.

I'd retreat to my room and lock the door, praying that flimsy piece of wood was enough to keep the chaos on the other side where it belonged.

I wasn't safe. And my mom… well, she wasn't present enough—emotionally, mentally, spiritually—to see the trauma detonating around me. Or inside me.

It was during one of her absences that everything changed. I was about 14 or 15, and Nick was basically an adult. He often had friends over for nights that were filled with drugs, drinking, and generalized fuckery, standard shitshow kind of stuff. The people he brought around—some his age, others even older—felt dangerous, almost predatory. The level of general creepiness they exuded made my skin crawl. These nights left me feeling isolated, trapped in a space that was meant to be home but had become a nightmare. One night stands out more vividly than the others. His friends had grown more aggressive, urging me to drink and try drugs, some of them paying more attention to me than appropriate, the kind of attention that makes your stomach knot with fear. Their abuse damaged me, and I still have the hidden bruises to prove it. On that one night, somehow they'd decided in their drug-crazed state that I wasn't really me, like in the movie *Invasion of the Body Snatchers*, so they were full-on trying to hurt me.

I barricaded myself in my bedroom, hoping it would offer some kind of sanctuary, but this only seemed to provoke them further. My heart raced as I pushed my dresser against the door, praying it would hold. They pounded on my door, taunting me, growing louder and more violent. It was scary as fuck. I was overcome with the realization I was helpless. I hid under my bed and called my best friend, Christy, in tears. I didn't know what else to do. I thought I was going to die.

Christy kept me on the phone, her voice steadying me as best as it could, promising that help was on its way. I stayed under my bed, hugging myself tightly, trying to drown out the chaos echoing down the hallway. I don't know how long I stayed there, shaking and sobbing, feeling utterly alone. Then, finally, Christy told me to go to my window. Her father was there, waiting to help me. The memory of that moment is hazy, yet I can still recall the overwhelming relief as I crawled out my window and into his arms. I didn't understand it at the time, but that single act changed the course of my life. I never spent another night in that house.

Once my dad had been made aware of the environment I was in, he and Christy's parents made arrangements for me to live with them moving forward so that my mom could focus on healing herself and hopefully helping my brother. From that day forward, I had a new beginning, away from the chaos—a real chance to find whatever normalcy might exist for me. Sadly, the nightmares that I faced during those years did not quite let me go, haunting me for many years to come.

Which Life Is My Real One?

The McCann's and my dad worked out a plan that had me bouncing between Florida and Kuwait like some kind of diplomatic ping-pong ball with abandonment issues. Nothing says "normal childhood" like a bi-continental identity crisis. The logic? I needed to rebuild a stable relationship with my father. I had a lot of mistrust and resentment for both of my parents that needed mending. But it was with the McCann's that I learned how to be in a family. I didn't just hang out at the McCann house—I moved in. Like, *officially*. They cleared out a spare room that had been doing time as a box graveyard, and Ms. Laura—my unofficial super mom and reigning queen of quiet heroics—took me shopping to make it mine. She didn't just give me a place to sleep. She gave me a space to *exist.*

We turned that room into a teenage fever dream of safety and self-expression. Pink floral bedding, beautiful wooden furniture, soft lighting that didn't scream "interrogation," and shelves lined with the kinds of delicate stuffed animals and dolls you'd expect to find in a vintage tea party. Some of them were even inherited from my grandmother—sweet, sentimental, cozy.

And then there was the window. Where most girls might have put a dream catcher or a cute motivational quote, I had a Tickle Me Elmo dangling by a noose. Just swingin' there among the soft plushies and porcelain smiles like some kind of warning: Abandon hope, all ye who enter this hormonal hellscape.

Yep. I was totally well-adjusted.

Christy loved me for my weirdness—full-on, no notes—and still tells the story of how, while most kids beg for a puppy, she begged for a little sister and got me instead. "Mom, can I keep her?" she asked. Joke's on her—they actually did.

Living with the McCann's was, unexpectedly, one of the best things that could've happened to me. Satellite Beach wasn't exactly the epicenter of cultural excitement, but I fit in there in a way I hadn't anywhere else. The school had just over 800 kids and sat close to Patrick Air Force Base, so most of us were the human version of carry-on luggage—frequent flyers, used to hellos and goodbyes. I was no longer the odd one out, just one of the many weirdos with a suitcase full of stories.

For once, I was thriving. Straight A's, varsity sports, and editor of the sports page in the school newspaper. I was checking all the boxes like I was training for a life in high-achieving emotional suppression.

But under the gold stars and achievements, I was still quietly unraveling. I was *so* desperate not to be a burden that I made perfectionism my emotional support animal. Up at 5 a.m., I'd cook breakfast, shower, and get dressed before anyone else was even awake—like some overachieving ghost who just wanted to stay out of everyone's way. I had finally found a home that didn't require me to pack up and vanish—and I was terrified they'd realize I came with emotional baggage and a carry-on full of unresolved trauma.

Then, just when everything seemed settled, I'd jump back into a completely different world—Kuwait. There were no kids my age, unless you count the 19-to-22-year-old Marine security guards, who were basically grown-up teenagers with muscles and bad jokes. We didn't live on the embassy compound; we lived in an apartment smack in the middle of Kuwait City. No neighborhood kids to run around with, just me and the adults. My version of high school parties? Bartending at embassy functions at 17 and getting life advice from diplomatic drunks. I aged in dog years. But weirdly, I loved it. Kuwait was my favorite place on earth—like, if I had to do a "Where's Waldo" of my best self, I'd find her there, standing behind a makeshift bar at a NATO mixer, blending vodka and validation.

My dad and I actually started healing. We talked about all the hard stuff—how I'd blamed him for not knowing what was happening back home, how I'd projected all my pain onto him like an emotional overhead projector. He was nothing like the villain I'd made up in my head. He was soft-spoken, diplomatic, and damn good at what he did. By the time I hit 18 or 19, I hated myself for ever hating him. I had spent so long building up this fantasy world where my mom was perfect, and my brother and I were inseparable, that I couldn't admit I might've had something better right in front of me all along. I guess I thought being a grown-up made him immune—like adulthood came with an emotional hazmat suit and a permanent "I'm fine" sticker. Turns out, being a dad doesn't come with immunity to the emotional shitstorm that is life. I forgot he was still human—bleeding quietly while I was screaming into the void.

And if dads don't come unbreakable, neither do moms. I spent years hating her for falling apart, never realizing she was handed a life with no instruction manual and a ticking time bomb in her chest. I wanted her to be whole, to be soft, to be safe—but she was just trying not to drown. It took nearly twenty years of wreckage, silence, and swallowing my own bitterness before we clawed our way to something that finally resembled a relationship. The one I always needed. The one we both deserved.

When I was in Kuwait, it felt like I was living the life I could've had all along: desert parties at amazing luxurious tents called "diwaniyahs" that looked like deleted scenes from *Aladdin*, spontaneous trips to Egypt with my dad like, "Hey, wanna hit the Nile before we go back to America?" It was magic. It was intoxicating. It was infuriating. Because as soon as I got settled, I'd get yanked back into the other timeline—Sweet Valley Fucking High, population: confusion.

I didn't know who I was supposed to be anymore. Diplomat's daughter or high school athlete? Bartender at embassy parties or prom queen? Kid or adult? It felt like I was starring in some *Twilight Zone* reboot—except there was no commercial break, and the lead actress was losing her damn mind.

And living that life in Kuwait? It forced me to grow up fast. Like, *fast-fast.* One day I was a teen wreckage trying to pass geometry, the next I had the freedom to do what I wanted, when I wanted, with barely any guardrails. I learned how to hold a conversation with adults twice my age, navigate international events, and read a room like a trained hostage negotiator. My emotional intelligence leveled up out of sheer necessity. But somewhere in that process, I forgot something kind of crucial: I was still a kid—and a pretty messed-up one at that. Inside, I was still that abandoned, scared, overachieving little girl trying to outrun her own shadow in heels too big for her soul.

But even as I loved the cinematic version of my life in an exotic desert oasis, I felt this ache, this constant low hum of *wrongness.* Because with every switch of scenery, I had to switch personas, too. I had become fluent in code-swapping between two worlds that didn't overlap. In one, I was the driven high school kid who never cried and always overachieved; in the other, I was an adult-shaped teenager learning how to hold her own in rooms filled with power suits and politics.

And yeah, we've been here before—but this wasn't just a fun "she's-so-worldly" montage. This was when the personality fracture began. When I started to feel like I wasn't really *any* of these people—just a collection of performances held together with GPA scores and a fake smile.

It was like being the lead in two different shows airing in parallel universes. One was all rah-rah high school tropes, the other was a diplomatic drama with desert landscapes and emotional repression. And me? I was stuck somewhere in the commercial break, trying to remember which lines were mine. Every time I switched locations, I had to kill off a version of myself to make room for the next.

Two Dads, Two Universes

While my relationship with my biological dad was more like a best friend with a diplomatic passport, Brian McCann—my adopted dad—was pure Air Force energy wrapped in authority and a pair of Oakleys. Brian was an Air Force master sergeant who didn't *ask* you to get out of bed—he launched you out of it. Literally. I once tried to buy myself a minute with a groggy, "Hold on," and before I could finish the sentence, he was hauling me up and throwing me in the pool like a human grenade with a lesson to learn. I learned.

He was no-nonsense, intense, and allergic to bullshit—but he gave me structure, which I didn't even realize I was starving for. He also gave me Dairy Queen, extra gummy bears, and Wendy's after every track meet, which, let's be honest, was probably my love language. And the man showed up for me. When I said I wanted to pole vault—something girls at our school didn't even do—he and my coach didn't just say "go for it." They went full throttle. He partnered with my pops and bought me a bright pink competition pole named Ms. Stic—because of course she had a name. He shipped me off to a specialty summer camp the summer of my junior year so I could "improve my skills," which is parent-speak for "We fully support your delusional belief that you might one day make the Olympic team."

And listen—pole vault camp? That was a fever dream. A bunch of teenagers flinging themselves into the sky with long sticks like deranged circus trainees, supervised by coaches who pretended this was normal. Meanwhile, I'm over here with Ms. Stic, the pink diva of vaulting, convinced I was destined for greatness, or at least trying not to break my collarbone.

At school, I was the only high-school girl sprinting down the runway with a giant, twelve-foot pink pole. The teenage-boy humor machine practically short-circuited. The jokes wrote themselves. Every day, some 16-year-old boy would make a comment that would get him immediately canceled today: "Nice pole, Jessica," or "Wow, she really knows how to handle that thing," followed by wheezing laughter and chest thumping, like they'd invented the concept of sexual innuendo.

And then, naturally, the poles started breaking.

If you've never heard the crack of a pole snapping mid-vault, imagine God slapping a pool noodle against a wall while screaming—equal parts terrifying and humiliating. But to the boys? This was an Oscar-level comedy. Every time one snapped, they'd lose their shit—*Oh no, she broke another one*—as if I were out there snapping dicks in half for sport.

Never mind the fact that pole breakage is a massive pain in the ass—expensive, inconvenient, and a constant reminder that at any moment, you might get impaled while launching your body into the sky on a glorified fishing rod. But teenage boys aren't known for nuance. Teenage boys are idiots.

Meanwhile, I kept my focus and kept jumping, determined to make gravity my bitch and humiliate physics along the way. While I was out there telling the laws of physics to "eat it" every day (a bold and dumb strategy), I had two men supporting me like my own personal pit crew. Between Brian on the ground and my father me from a distance, I was enabled, funded, and believed in—three things I didn't even know I was allowed to expect.

But even with all that, I couldn't stop bouncing between extremes. In one world, I was the daughter of a man who spoke in careful, measured tones and treated diplomacy like an art form. In the other, I was being shaped by a man who believed in discipline, endurance, and showing up no matter what.

It was like I had two dads from two different planets—and I was constantly shapeshifting to survive in each atmosphere, never wanting to let either of them down. Now that I had them, I never wanted to lose them.While both of them gave me parts of what I needed, I never quite figured out how to hold both truths at the same time: That I was loved, but still wildly, terrifyingly lost.

Breaking Point

It was junior year, and on paper, I was killing it: Sports, grades, achievements—check, check, check. But inside? I was about two skipped meals and a sideways glance away from a full emotional implosion. It happened in weightlifting class of all places, because of course it did. Nothing says "mental health crisis" like gym shorts and the smell of Axe body spray. I was sitting there next to my friend Dave, trying to act normal—whatever that meant anymore—when he looked at me out of the blue and asked, "What's it like for you? You're always here. Then you're there. Then here… then there. How do you cope?"

I'd never heard anyone describe my life that way—like motion itself was the thing eating me alive. His words landed softly, but they cracked something loud inside me. No one had ever so bluntly pointed out the whiplash of my existence before. And I wasn't coping.

I don't know what it was about that moment—maybe the way he said it, maybe the fact that he asked at all. I opened my mouth to answer and instead, I just…broke. I started crying, hard. Like, ugly crying, a can't-stop, can't-breathe, snot-and-tears-everywhere level meltdown. I don't even think I responded. I dissolved into full emotional collapse, no dignity, no composure, just the kind of grief that rips you to the core and drags you to your knees, whether you want to go or not.

The next thing I knew, someone called for my pole vaulting coach, who showed up like a guardian angel disguised as a track coach, the type of mentor I wish every kid got at least once in their life. When he walked in, I could barely lift my head. He gathered me up—gentle but sure—and led me out of the classroom. I followed him because I didn't know what else to do. Because everything hurt and I was so, so tired.

He took me to see the school counselor. She sat down across from me, studying my face in a way no one really had before. Then she said quietly, "We need to call Laura McCann."

That's when the panic hit.

I didn't want to call her. Laura was the head of a large home loan company. She was busy, important, and professional, and I was determined not to be the teenage trainwreck who got her pulled out of a board meeting, just because I couldn't keep my shit together in weightlifting class. I started hyperventilating, sobbing harder, begging them not to call. My whole body screamed, *Do not be a burden. Do not be a problem. Do not be the reason someone's day gets worse.*

They called her anyway. And she came.

What happened next is something I didn't fully understand at the time. Laura didn't walk in angry. She didn't look embarrassed. She didn't glare or sigh or make me feel like I'd ruined her day. She looked at me, really looked at me, and something in her face softened. She put her hand on my back, steady and warm, and took me straight to a therapist. No hesitation. No questions that felt like accusations. Just quiet determination. Just love.

In that moment, something undeniable settled into place, the kind of truth that doesn't need an explanation, you just know it's real: A mother's love doesn't hinge on DNA. It's not inherited. It's chosen, shown, proven. And she was choosing me.

I don't remember much after that. I only remember crying for what felt like hours while adults talked around me in low voices. Medication. Therapy. Safety. The word "depression" floating in the air like an allegation I was afraid to accept. But Laura stayed. She didn't leave me. She didn't hand me off. She stayed. And something shifted.

A tiny seed planted itself in the middle of all that fear—a thought I didn't dare believe, but couldn't quite push away: Maybe I wasn't being abandoned. Maybe I was being held. Maybe I wasn't beyond saving after all.

That breakdown felt like punishment, like proof that I was too much, too fragile, too broken. It cracked me open. It was devastating. It was humiliating. It felt like dying. But for the first time, the light had somewhere to go. I had spent so long trying to hold myself together, convinced that if anyone saw the truth of what I carried, they'd turn away.

Laura didn't turn away. And that changed everything.

It didn't fix everything at once, of course. I wasn't suddenly reborn into a chill, emotionally stable teen goddess, but I wasn't carrying the weight alone anymore, either. The people that mattered knew. And instead of rejecting me, they leaned in. They didn't flinch at my mess. They kept showing up.

That small shift—that feeling of being seen and not sent packing—started to rewire me. I didn't have to white-knuckle my way through every day pretending to be fine. I still tried, don't get me wrong. Perfectionism was still my security blanket. People-pleasing was basically my part-time job. But now, I had people in my corner. And I let them help, a little.

I also started taking therapy seriously—not just showing up, but talking, owning the fact that I'd been through some deeply fucked-up things. Admitting I wasn't okay didn't kill me—it might have actually been the thing that kept me alive. And medication? Not a personality eraser, just a volume knob, turning down the screaming so I could finally think straight.

That year was the beginning of a different kind of fight. Not the survival-mode, power-through-it battle I was used to, but the hard, boring, deeply uncomfortable work of healing.

Fast forward to senior year: I was prom queen. No, seriously. Me. The emotional disaster in a hoodie. Crowned. It was a rare occasion when I realized that my differences—the weirdness, the pain, the sharp edges—might actually be what made me special. I still felt like I had to be perfect, but I started to think that maybe, just maybe, I was going to be okay.

Almost Okay

After graduation, I did what you're *supposed* to do when you've made it through the chaos and crowned your healing with a plastic prom queen tiara—I went to college. I decided to stay in Florida and go to UCF. I had a full-ride scholarship between academics and pole vaulting. Christy—my human anchor and chosen sister—was going there too. We got an apartment together, and I thought, *Maybe this is it. Maybe this is where things finally even out.*

I was hopeful. Like, suspiciously so. My dad, still gently trying to nudge me toward some semblance of balance and life as an 18-year-old, suggested I join a sorority. I rolled my eyes so hard I nearly gave myself a concussion—but I did it. I met various sisterhoods that day, but against every stereotype I'd built in my head, the sorority I chose, who chose me too, wasn't some glossy, packaged sisterhood you buy your way into. It wasn't shallow or rehearsed or competitive. I met a group of women who were wildly different from one another—different backgrounds, different strengths, different flaws—and somehow, that mosaic made each of them more beautiful. They weren't versions of who I thought I should be; they were entirely themselves. And that alone felt radical to me.

And this part matters: I'm not taking anything away from the friends I'd already made in high school. Many of them are still in my life, still woven into who I am. But these new girls…they met me at a very specific moment. A moment when I was shedding old armor and relearning how to be a person in the world. They didn't know my backstory, my bruises, my breakdowns. They didn't carry my history, and in a way, that made it easier to breathe.

It felt like a clean slate—not because I wanted to erase who I'd been, but because, for the first time, I got to introduce myself without the weight of everything I'd survived. And for a while, that felt like freedom.

I was also one of UCF's first female pole vaulters, which gave me something to hold onto, something that still made me feel strong and special, like I was becoming someone I could actually root for. But the shift from a small, beachside high school to a 40,000-student university hit me like a bus. I went from being known and understood to feeling completely lost in a sea of backpacks, opinions, and existential dread.

And then there was the culture shock. It was 1998, and people had opinions about the Middle East—and not the nuanced, informed kind. I found myself in heated debates with anti-Arab assholes who assumed anyone who'd lived in Kuwait must have terrorist pen pals and a Koran under their pillow. Suddenly, everything that made me unique back home made me *suspect* here. I felt like a walking stereotype with a target on my back.

Just when I thought I'd adjusted to all that, I blew out my knee. No more pole vaulting. No more required 5 a.m. three-mile runs and structure. No more identity. Just like that, the one thing tethering me to some sense of stability was gone. I started spiraling—quietly, at first. A few drinks here and there to take the edge off. Some skipped classes. A lot of nights staring at the ceiling wondering why I still felt like a fraud in my own life. I thought I had left that fragile girl far behind, but the version of me I had been building, the one who was confident, capable, and completely fine, was slipping through my fingers.

Losing Myself

I wasn't falling apart in some dramatic, headline-worthy way. There was no epic rock bottom, no montage of solo vodka shots and flunked exams. It was quieter than that. Slower. More… slippery.

I started losing myself in the *performance* of normal.

At UCF, everyone seemed to know who they were and what they were doing. They had matching dorm room sets and dream internships and parents who called just to say hi. I wanted that. I wanted to blend in—to be just another bubbly blonde college girl with a full social calendar and no visible scars.

So I played the part.

I went to the parties. I smiled through the hangovers. I laughed a little too loud, danced a little too hard, and said yes to everything that felt like belonging. It wasn't about drinking—I didn't need alcohol to get lost. I was already fading. I just wanted to be wanted. To be liked. To be *normal.*

And honestly? I was good at it. I could be the life of the party, the funny one, the chill girl who didn't take herself too seriously. But underneath all that charm was a growing emptiness I didn't have the tools to name. The girl everyone liked wasn't really me. She was just a costume I zipped up every morning and hoped no one would notice didn't quite fit.

In Kuwait, I felt older than I was. In college, I felt *smaller*—like I'd regressed into someone desperate for approval, afraid of silence, terrified of not being chosen. I wasn't drinking to forget. I was partying to disappear.

And slowly, I did.

I stopped going to class as much. I stopped calling home. I stopped checking in with myself. I was too busy trying to be fun, pretty, effortless. The perfect college version of myself. Which, spoiler alert, doesn't exist—even for the girls who *look* like they have it all together on Instagram before Instagram was even a thing.

And then, right in the middle of all that carefully constructed chaos, came the email that shattered it all.

Plot Twist

I don't remember what day it was or what I had for dinner or what song was playing in the background—but I remember the email. It was from a family member. And it wasn't kind. I don't remember every word, but I remember the feeling—the way it hit like a slap across the face from someone you forgot was still watching. The gist? That I was selfish. That my mother was falling apart while I was off "living my life." That I didn't care. That I never came home. That I had abandoned the person who gave birth to me, and wasn't that just *so* convenient? It was a character assassination written in passive-aggressive italics. And the worst part? Somewhere deep down, I believed them.

It didn't matter that I was barely holding myself together. That I was still trying to process years of trauma I hadn't even begun to name. That I was clinging to this shiny new version of life like it might finally erase the past. One email, and suddenly I was the villain again. And the timing? Of course it had to hit on a night when everything else felt okay. I'd been out with my two best friends, laughing, pretending—maybe even *believing*—that I was just like everyone else. For a few hours, I let myself exist without the weight. I felt...light. Human. Safe.

Then I checked my email.

And just like that, I wasn't a girl in an apartment after a night out. I was a failure. A fraud. A ghost with hollow eyes and no purpose.

I finished the night like nothing was wrong. Smiled. Laughed. Hugged them goodbye. Made sure they believed the performance. And then I walked into the bathroom, locked the door, and tried to end it. A full bottle of pain pills. Some vodka. A razor. A silence so loud it practically screamed.

I wasn't doing it for attention. I wasn't doing it as a cry for help. I truly, deeply believed the world would be better off without me in it. That I had done enough damage. That I had already taken up too much space.

The only reason I'm alive is because of Samantha.

Samantha, who had already started driving back home but felt a gut instinct—that sixth sense you can't explain. She turned around. Drove back. Found me. Manhandled the door open. Called for help. And saved my life.

I don't remember much after that. Just flashes. Stomach pumps. The burn of humiliation. And then...my dad, sitting beside me, looking older, more broken. He had been in Kuwait when they called. He got on a plane and flew halfway across the world. And he was there before I even woke up. That's how far down I had gone. And how far someone still came to get me.

The Fallout

I woke up in a hospital bed with a foggy head and a father who looked like he'd aged a decade in a day. His eyes were red. His face was pale. And all I could think was, *What the fuck have I done to him?*

I was being held under the Baker Act—a Florida law that allows doctors to hold you involuntarily in a mental health facility for up to 72 hours if they think you're a danger to yourself or others. Spoiler alert: I had checked all the boxes.

The room was cold. The air smelled like bleach and despair. I was wearing socks with those grippy little treads on the bottom and a hospital gown that felt like punishment. I couldn't eat. I didn't want to talk. I definitely didn't want visitors. But they came anyway. People kept showing up—

friends and people who loved me. And I wouldn't see any of them. I couldn't. I was too embarrassed. Too angry. Too…numb. There's a special kind of shame that comes after surviving something you didn't *want* to survive. It sticks to your skin like sweat you can't shower off.

In my head, I was still blaming everyone else. I wasn't ready to hold the mirror up yet. I was thinking, *How did they let me get this way? Why didn't anyone stop it? Why didn't they fix it sooner?* It was easier than admitting that I didn't know how to fix myself.

Once I was released, my dad took me back to Kuwait. Not because I was magically healed, but because we didn't know what else to do. It was around the holidays, but there was no cheer—just shattered Christmas wishes and candy-coated Xanax served up in place of sugar cookies and cocoa. The lights were twinkling, the decorations were up, but everything felt hollow—like the world had dressed itself up for a party I no longer had the will to attend. December came and went in a medicated blur.

My dad was broken. I couldn't see it clearly at the time—I was too deep in my own haze—but looking back now, he was unraveling. Quietly.

Painfully. Watching your child try to die will do that to a person. And I hadn't fully grasped what I had done. Not just to me. But to *him.*

And just when things started to level off—just when I started to think maybe I could coast through the fog until the pain wore off—I did it again. The thing about surviving a suicide attempt is people start watching you like you're made of glass. Like one wrong move, one bad thought, and you'll shatter. I didn't feel fragile, though. I felt… gone. Like I was haunting my own life.

I was still in Kuwait, but it didn't feel like *my* Kuwait anymore, not the place where I'd once thrived, not the place of spontaneous trips and diplomatic parties. Now it was just an apartment I hid inside, curtains drawn, trying not to think too hard or feel too much. I wasn't in pain, exactly. I wasn't anything. I was a flatline in human form—going through the motions, taking my meds, pretending to exist. I didn't want to die… but I also didn't really want to be here. I was in that in-between place where you're not crying for help, you're just whispering it into a void and hoping someone hears.

And one night, I didn't whisper. I acted.

It wasn't as dramatic. Not like the first time. I slit my wrists again, but it was slower. Softer. Less "end it all" and more "can somebody *please* see how much I'm drowning?"

I don't remember doing it. I remember coming to, sitting on the floor, staring down at my wrists like they belonged to someone else. I remember the blood. I remember the confusion. But the act itself? Gone. Like I'd sleepwalked through it. My dad found me or maybe I had cried out for help. I don't know.

He said I looked like a zombie—blank eyes, slurred voice, completely disconnected. I turned to him and said, "Daddy, I don't know what I just did."

And I didn't. I truly didn't. It was like my body had taken over in the absence of my mind. I was on so much medication that I couldn't tell reality from reflex. I was gone—and yet still here. Which, somehow, felt worse.

It wasn't as severe this time, physically. But emotionally? It carved a new kind of scar. This time, I couldn't blame it on a bad night or a cruel email or a bottle of pills. This time, it was me...quietly slipping under, hoping someone would notice before it was too late.

And thank God—he did.

The Year I Could Breathe

After the second attempt, I stayed in Kuwait instead of returning to school. I took a medical withdrawal and hit pause on everything that had been spiraling out of control. I told myself it was temporary—just a little time to catch my breath, maybe figure out how to stop wanting to disappear all the time. I needed to stop pretending I was okay and actually *become* okay. I needed to heal somewhere that didn't carry the scent of failure.

Within a few months—thanks to therapy, a cocktail of meds, and the spiritual CPR that only my beloved Kuwait could give—I began to live again, like *actually* live. I started working again at the embassy, started teaching Tae Bo and yoga, and somehow—because the universe has a wicked sense of humor—ended up co-hosting a morning workout segment on Kuwait's local TV show.

I mean, imagine flipping channels and landing on *me*, cheerfully guiding viewers through sun salutations with freshly bandaged trauma just out of frame. But somehow...it worked. I was showing up. Smiling. Laughing. Feeling.

And, of course, I met a boy.

There's *always* a boy. He was kind. Steady. He made me believe love didn't have to hurt, didn't have to leave. We fell into it fast and hard, and I let myself dream. We fell in love in that all-consuming way you do when you're 20-something. *I could live here forever*, I thought. This could be my life—sunrises over the Gulf, desert parties, a soft place to land in someone's arms.

But life—reliably cruel—had other plans. My dad's diplomatic term was ending. He was retiring, which meant I couldn't stay. No more work visa. No more co-host gig. No more fairy tale. It all fell apart with one bureaucratic deadline.

Everything felt ruined. Again.

The thought of returning to the States—to the site of my pain, my failures, my shame—was suffocating. I wasn't just terrified. I was gutted. I had just started to *live,* and now I was being asked to start over. Again. Everything I had built during that year—my routine, my peace, my fragile hope—wasn't strong enough to survive re-entry. And deep down, I think I knew it.

Leaving Kuwait felt like the universe grabbed the heart I'd just spent a year sewing back together and hurled it into the desert with a casual, "Good luck out there," as if anything survives in 120-degree heat except regret and ghosts we never quite shake.

I packed up my little oasis of healing, said goodbye to the boy I carried in my heart for years to come, and got on a plane back to the scene of the crime. And let me tell you—re-entering the US after a year of hard-won recovery was like parachuting into a burning building with a note that said, "Try not to die this time."

The minute I landed, I could feel the cracks forming again. The air was heavier. The silence was louder. And suddenly, I was just another blonde girl in a crowd, stripped of the identity I'd carved out for myself overseas. Time to face my demons and those I had hurt and left behind. Just me, my American passport, and the sneaking suspicion that I had already peaked.

It didn't take long for the darkness to catch up. I tried to do the things—school, socializing, pretending I hadn't just left the only place that had ever made me feel whole. But everything felt dull and performative. I was going through the motions, one missed class turned into two missed classes. One day in bed turned into a week. The old voices came back, louder and meaner this time, whispering things like, *"You fucked it all up. Again."*

I tried reaching out to my mom again, because part of me still clung to the fantasy that maybe this time would be different. It wasn't. Cue the emotional whiplash and fresh wounds ripped open like they had just been waiting for me to come back and scratch the scab.

There were boys, of course—because distraction is easier than healing. And some of them were kind, but most of them saw the version of me I *pretended* to be and didn't care enough to look any deeper. Being used by someone who never really saw you is its own special brand of erasure. And I felt erased—by men, life, shattered goals, by my own reflection, by the universe itself. So I did what I knew. I shut down. I got quiet. I disappeared in plain sight.

And then, I tried to disappear for real.

The third attempt didn't come with theatrics. It wasn't a breakdown or a crisis. It wasn't even a moment of passion or desperation. It was quiet. Detached. A decision made from a place so numb it barely felt like choosing at all.

It was a slow slide into that place where pain and peace become indistinguishable—where the hurting is so constant that the idea of stopping feels merciful. And the truth is, there's nothing more terrifying than reaching a point where the thing that can end you feels gentle.

There was no note. No plan. Just exhaustion. Like I'd been trying so hard to be everything—strong, healed, whole—and I was just… done.

When I woke up, my dad was there again. He looked different. Not just worried. Not just tired. Wrecked. Like something inside him had already mourned me and was terrified it would have to do it again; begging the universe not to take his baby girl. One look at his face and I knew—whatever I thought I was sparing the world from, I was wrong. I wasn't eliminating a burden. I was ripping holes in the people who loved me.

I had spent my whole life trying not to take up space, trying not to need anything, trying not to be a problem. And somehow, in the middle of all that effort, I had become the heaviest weight they were all carrying.

And for the first time, I didn't want to die. I couldn't stand the thought of hurting them anymore. That was the shift—the quiet, brutal, I-have-to-live realization. That was the last time.

Barbie's House of Horrors: Meet the Barbies in My Head (Spoiler Alert—They're Not OK)

The Origin Story

So here's the deal: I bottomed out—three strikes and somehow still breathing—and all the pieces of my life blurred together into this strange in-between space. When I try to map the timeline now, it's like looking at watercolors left out in the rain. What I do remember is this: There was a stretch of time when everything felt unbearable… and then a stretch when things finally loosened their grip on my throat.

For me, Kuwait lives in that latter category. Not in a neat-before-or-after way—more like a pause in the chaos. Therapy, Xanax, workouts, and a small circle of friends who didn't care about the curated young-adult facades everyone was busy maintaining gave me my first real breath in years. Kuwait was my bubble of borrowed oxygen.

But bubbles don't last. They never do.

Eventually, I found myself back in Florida, facing the fallout of everything I'd tried so hard to outrun. Florida was brutal. Half the people looked at me like I might self-destruct in aisle five of Publix; the other half were quietly angry that I hadn't kept my crisis more… convenient. Meanwhile, I was dragging around a suitcase full of guilt, paranoia, and unanswered questions. Who still likes me? Who thinks I'm unstable? Who's waiting for the sequel?

And no, there's no magical post-crisis glow-up. It's not *cue the holiday miracle.* It's more like *dragging yourself uphill in wet flip-flops, praying the strap doesn't snap.*

Somewhere in all of that mess—twenty-one, exhausted, ashamed, and trying to act like a functional person—I went back to school and stitched together College Barbie: Smiling, steady, totally "fine." Everyone treated me differently, so I started acting differently, too. That's when the Barbie alter-egos started showing up.

With Madison—my ride-or-die—I became Keep-Your-Shit-Together Barbie, whether I felt steady or not. With everyone else, I adjusted, adapted, and shapeshifted. I curated versions of myself depending on who needed what. I was a different Barbie for every audience—collect them all, just don't ask who the hell the original was supposed to be.

It was pure survival, plastic-wrapped, and the only one paying the price was me.

After a couple of years of being everyone's "Choose Your Own Jessica," I was running on fumes. That's when I met Marco. On paper, he looked like the upgrade I didn't know I needed: A little older, confident, handy, gave off the vibe that he had his shit together. In reality? I was lost. I didn't trust myself; I didn't know who the hell I even was. So, of course, I fell for him. Hard.

We dated on and off for about three years, and I quickly realized that instead of being *a* Jessica, I became *his* Jessica. He wanted a certain version of me and I played it. Marco wasn't just controlling; he was a masterclass in mental manipulation.

At first it was "just" intimidation—slamming doors, running at me so I'd trip, then gaslighting me with, "You did that to yourself. You're dumb." (Creative, right?)

Then came the aggression. He once kicked my dog across the room and told me if I touched him, he'd kill him. That was the level of control. And yes, my friends saw it. Two of my best friends at the time staged full-on interventions, begging me to get out. But here's the thing about toxic relationships: You don't realize how deep you're in until the quicksand is at your neck.

Eventually, it escalated—it always does. One day, Marco pushed me against a wall hard enough to crack my skull. That was the "last straw." But really, the last straw had been a thousand straws ago—the part where I'd already lost friends, lost versions of myself, and was laughing off everything like some broken sitcom character.

The real Jessica, the one I'd been trying to piece back together, was gone. In her place were the old survival versions I never wanted to meet again: The quiet one, the careful one, the girl who remembered exactly how to shrink herself, soften herself, and disappear herself to stay safe. Not because she wanted to, but because terror is a language the body never forgets. Terror didn't teach me new tricks, it reminded me of the ones I'd hoped I'd never need again.

Work became my escape hatch. I got a job at a mortgage company and clawed my way up. By 25, I was pulling six figures. I even bought my first house—a total fixer-upper, but mine. Marco, of course, found his way back in. He dangled the "handy boyfriend" act, promising to help me refurbish it, playing nice until I let him move in. That's when the real shitshow started. Suddenly, everything was, "You wouldn't have this house if it weren't for me." Excuse me? I signed the damn mortgage. But that was Marco's's specialty: Twisting reality until I didn't know which way was up.

On the outside, I looked like I had it all—sports, parties, friends, a booming career. On the inside, I was living in fear. During my last year with Marco, I wasn't myself. I moved through life hollow, disconnected, and compliant in ways that didn't even feel like choices anymore. I became whatever version of me people needed because it was easier than facing what was happening behind closed doors.

When I was alone, I felt nothing. And when I did feel something, it was unpredictable and out of place—anger at moments that should have been joyful, numbness at moments that should have broken me open. Sometimes nothing at all, for months. It scared me so much that I genuinely wondered if something was fundamentally wrong with me, if I was incapable of real emotion anymore.

I remember researching symptoms late at night, trying to figure out whether I was becoming a sociopath, because I didn't understand how else a person could feel so empty while their life was falling apart. It wasn't a joke. It was terror. I had no idea that trauma could hollow you out so completely that you start questioning your own humanity.

My friends weren't blind. They saw what was happening. Two of my best friends flat out said, "We can't watch this anymore. Either you get out, or we're stepping back, because seeing you like this is breaking us, too." They were trying to pull me out of the quicksand, but I was too far down to grab the rope.

The breaking point came when my adopted mom was dying. My sister called: It was organ failure. She was in the hospital an hour and a half away. I tried to leave, but Marco had taken my keys. I begged, I showed him texts, I asked him to drive me. His response was a flat, chilling, "Yeah, right."

He thrived on being in control. It took me two and a half hours to get out of that house. I made it to my mom eventually, but I'll never forget that my focus had been on fighting him instead of being fully present with her. That guilt stayed with me long after he was out of my life.

I finally got him out—cops, 30 days of "squatters' rights" nonsense, and friends rolling up in trucks on eviction day like they were bracing for a showdown. Finally, Marco was gone.

On paper, things looked golden. I was 26, with a career ahead of me, making good money, two majors and a minor under my belt. I was throwing parties, surrounded by friends. But inside? Empty. The lights were on, but no one was home.

I'd always pictured depression as sadness—weeping, collapsing, unable to get out of bed. But this was different. This was numbness. Disassociation. Months of feeling like I was watching my own life from the outside. My friends would ask, "Why aren't you crying?" and I genuinely believed I was—just not in any way they could see.

Depression comes in many forms, and this one was quiet, hollow, and suffocating. I eventually returned to counseling, and thank God I did. Because here's what I know now: Depression isn't something you beat once. You don't graduate from it. Sometimes you have to keep going back to therapy, whether it's your first time or your fiftieth. It's like recovery—you can always find yourself starting over, and there's no shame in picking up your Day One chip again.

While I was hiding my emotions from the people who loved me—terrified of worrying them, terrified of seeming unstable—I started picking up new hobbies that gave me reasons to be away. Poker. Sports leagues. Walks in parks. At first, I thought these were distractions. Later, I realized they were pieces of myself I hadn't been safe enough to show yet. My anger had a place on the field. My quiet had a place at the poker table. My calm showed up in nature.

By my thirties, I finally understood: I wasn't fracturing. I was surviving. I was letting different parts of myself breathe in the only ways I knew how. And maybe, just maybe, that was the real Jessica all along.

Good News! You're Probably Not a Fucking Psycho!

Take a breath. No, seriously. Right now. Because if you've made it to this point in the book, you've earned a moment when your body can unclench and your soul can stop waiting for the next emotional plot twist. This is where the tone shifts. This is where we move from *What the actual fuck?* to *Okay...what now?*

I didn't understand any of this back then. All I knew was that I felt like twelve different people holding hands inside one brain, and not a single one of them was sure who was in charge. If you've ever thought, *Why am I so many versions of myself?* I want you to hear me: You're not crazy. You're not broken. You're not morphing into a psychopath because Google says you checked five out of nine symptoms at 2 a.m. What you're experiencing is survival.

Trauma reshapes the mind. It doesn't always show up as tears or dramatic breakdowns. Sometimes it shows up as adaptation—the mind breaking itself into rooms so the pain doesn't flood the whole house at once.

It creates roles, personas, instincts. Not because something is wrong with you, but because something tried to destroy you, and your mind said, *Absolutely not. We're staying alive.*

Compartmentalization can look like being a different person with friends, family, partners, and coworkers, not because you're fake, but because each version of you is carrying a different piece of the load. It's your psyche distributing the weight so one part of you doesn't collapse. At different moments, we may find ourselves embodying different versions of who we are.

I eventually learned that all these versions of me weren't malfunctions. They were helpers. Parts of myself stepped forward when I needed a specific kind of strength, calm, detachment, humor, or fire. I call mine the Barbie Brigade—not because they're cute or plastic, but because giving them names helped me understand who was showing up and why. It turned chaos into a system. It gave shape to the parts of me I used to mistake for instability.

For example, when I walk into a boardroom, the version of me who takes over is unwavering, composed, and surgically focused. That's Boss Bitch Barbie—she's the one who makes decisions, not apologies. There are others, each with their own job. Each one a survival mechanism with a personality.

And here's the big revelation, the part that begins the "what now" part of this book: These personas weren't proof I was broken. They were proof I adapted. They were proof I endured. They were proof I stayed alive.

As for the rest of the chaos crew, well, here they come. There's the warm, nurturing one who knows how to comfort and care for others, even when she is barely holding her own shit together. Say hello to Hallmark Barbie, always ready to lend a kind word, supportive wisdom, and if that all fails, break out the bourbon! When life demands responsibility and strength, Big Girl Barbie steps up, shoulders the burdens, and keeps things moving. She hides her scars, swallows her tears, and gets shit done.

But let's not forget the less…shall we say…polished personas. Sometimes, when pushed to the edge, Shank-a-Bitch Barbie shows up. She's got zero patience and no time for nonsense, ready to throw down (figuratively, of course…most of the time).

Some Barbies stay hidden until things just get too overwhelming, like Emotional Meltdown Barbie, with her mascara running, the tears flowing, one Taylor Swift song away from a full-on breakdown. And don't forget Bourbon Barbie, who's never far behind, sipping her whiskey neat, finding solace in the bottom of a glass. These Barbies might not show their faces, but they're always there. Each member of my Barbie Brigade serves a purpose, helping me cope with the demands of trauma and everyday life.

These personas aren't inauthentic or fronts; rather, they represent different facets of ourselves that emerge in response to life's challenges. In a way, they are survival strategies. They're not masks as much as they are exaggerated versions of our reality, stepping in when we need a little extra help navigating the chaos. Over time, these fragmented versions of our identity can take on a life of their own, creating a complex, layered self that may be difficult to untangle.

While these personas are great at helping us navigate life, there's also the issue of figuring out who's actually in charge at any given moment. It's like you're running a one-person production with an ever-changing cast of characters. Boss Barbie might handle the professional stuff like a pro, but suddenly you're at a casual brunch, and she's barking out orders about mimosa refills. Or maybe Bourbon Barbie shows up to cope with some stress, and before you know it, she's trying to take over your 9 a.m. work meetings. It's easy to get so used to wearing these personas that it can be hard to figure out where they end and the real "you" begins.

For me, it's Barbie, probably because of my love for alliteration and let's face it, there are a lot of words that start with B! People unconsciously adopt all kinds of personas to cope, sometimes even modeling them after their favorite childhood characters. I mean, who hasn't channeled their inner Disney Princess when they need to play the role of graceful and calm under pressure? Or summoned Elsa energy when it's time to "let it go" and freeze out the drama in their lives?

Maybe you're more into Care Bears—because who wouldn't want to be Tenderheart Bear when the group needs some love and positivity? But watch out for Grumpy Bear, who's not afraid to let everyone know just how done they are with everything. And let's be real, when things get really tough, some of us go full Power Ranger, morphing into a color-coded warrior ready to tackle anything—complete with high kicks and dramatic poses.

I've noticed that the more I speak with people who have survived various forms of trauma, the more common it becomes to hear them express a deep connection with the idea of having multiple personalities. Many of them feel uneasy about it, wondering if something is seriously wrong with them. I know I certainly did. The fear that I was possibly demonstrating characteristics of a sociopath was real. But more on that later, campers.

People fear that these different personas might be a sign of dysfunction, rather than recognizing them for what they truly are: Powerful coping mechanisms. Instead of seeing these personalities as fractures or evidence that you are broken, embrace the reality that you have subconsciously developed a system that not only helps you survive but, in many cases, has allowed you to get to this point. Congratulations are in order! Celebrate yourself for the beautiful, magnificent specimen of a human being you are!

These personas aren't a weakness; they're evidence of the mind's incredible resilience and creativity, adapting to the chaos of trauma by crafting versions of the self that each fulfill a specific need.

If there's anything I know for sure, it's that trauma bends you into a different person, or many different people, all tangled together, until you don't know who you are. I became someone who had to be perfect, who had to succeed, even when my life felt like it was falling apart. Emotional Breakdown Barbie was under the surface of everything I did, even as I strived to be perfect. I got straight A's in school, even when I was screaming inside. I put so much pressure on myself to be the person everyone else needed me to be that I lost sight of who I needed to be, for myself and myself only.

My inner world might seem weird to other people, but it's the survival skill that's helped me fight for my life, professionally and personally. I became a successful entrepreneur. I made my own way in a male-dominated field. I made it to the other side of toxic relationships. I figured out who I really was and I embraced every fractured part of myself, until I became whole.

I didn't figure all this out overnight. Getting there was ugly, messy, chaotic, but I'm sharing this to prove that if I can get through the insane shitshows that kept playing throughout my life and pop out the other end, not just okay but kicking ass and thriving—well, sometimes—then you can, too.

Big Girl Barbie Owns Her Shit (Even When It's on Fire)

The Star of the Show

Now that you've met some of the Barbies rattling around in my head, let me introduce the headliner: Big Girl Barbie. She's the one who gets the most stage time, mostly because she's the only one who remembered to pack her big girl panties. She strutted out into the spotlight the minute I came back from Kuwait and realized I had to get my shit together. And while I'd *love* to tell you that was the hardest thing I've ever done, that would be a lie. Not because it wasn't hard—it was—but because life has handed me so many "hardest things ever" that I could fill a Top 40 countdown.

Leaving Kuwait felt like someone was yanking me out of my personal safe zone. It was my little bubble, my haven. Meanwhile, my dad had already bailed six months earlier, retired from the Foreign Service, and gone full cliché—moved to Florida. Except paradise wasn't exactly on the menu. He managed to fracture his back without realizing it, which is both a very "dad" thing to do and also explains why he flew home first. So there I was, clinging to Kuwait like it was my last lifeboat, while everyone else thought I should be frolicking in Florida. Plot twist: Florida wasn't paradise for me. Florida was where the demons lived. And oh, they were waiting.

So I crash-landed in my dad's guest room with a to-do list straight out of Dante's "Face Your Shit" Inferno. Priority number one: Finish school. Sports scholarships should have been my golden ticket, except, surprise, I'd already blown out my knee. One major surgery before Kuwait, four more after, and a "congratulations, you'll need a total replacement one day" punch card to show for it. Pole vaulting was out, but I still refused to retire my athlete card. I played soccer and football socially into my late thirties, because stubbornness is my version of cardio.

Enter Big Girl Barbie. She wasn't going to let me come back branded as "that weak girl who tried to kill herself three times." Nope. I dusted off my overachiever's playbook (the one I first tested with the McCann's) and went all in again. This time, I wasn't just proving to everyone else that I was okay. I was desperately trying to prove it to myself.

Case in point: That part-time gig at a mortgage company, run by what can only be described as a grown-up Dennis the Menace on speed. Nice guy, funny, but focus? Nonexistent. The man had a Cessna and a house in the Bahamas, and every Friday he'd just peace-out mid-deal like, "Bye, Jessica, I'll be drunk on a beach until Tuesday. Also, can you close these three loans? I'll throw in scuba gear."

And me? Like an idiot Barbie on Red Bull: "Yeah, sure, okay!"

One minute I'm saying we don't even do subprime loans, the next he's like, "Cool, can you get certified for subprime?" And what do I do? I actually go and get certified. Then the Series 7 license. Then insurance and annuities. Before long, I had every certification under the sun—paid for by my boss, who technically "ran" the company while I was the one keeping it from bursting into flames.

Big Girl Barbie was slaying—school by day, mortgages by night, juggling so hard I could've joined Cirque du Soleil. I bought my own house, moved out of Dad's guest room, and told myself I was thriving. I was also living with Marco at the time, so burying myself in work and school was just code for avoiding home.

All this happened while I was barely in my twenties. Identity? Fragmented. Relationship? Abusive. Yet I was overachieving like my life depended on it, which, honestly, maybe it did. Because here's the real kicker about Big Girl Barbie: She wasn't just about grades and paychecks. She was about taking ownership and refusing to let my demons eat me alive. Which brings me to my six-step action plan for owning your own life—demons and all—and loving who you've become.

Six Actions to Get Through Tough Times

One of the best things about Barbies—besides the fact that they never age, gain weight, or roll their eyes at you—is that you can make them do whatever the hell you want. That's the entire point, right? If they just sat there looking pretty, they'd be…well, Kardashians. My Barbies (the real plastic ones and the loud-mouthed ones in my head) aren't just decoration. They're coping mechanisms. They're little avatars for action and there is always power in action.

Action, my friends, is everything. You can't just sit back hoping your demons will get bored and wander off. They won't. You have to move, act, and try—sometimes boldly, sometimes badly, but always forward. That's where the real power lives.

Through the madness that's been my life, I've landed on six actions that have saved me more times than tequila and sarcasm combined. Think of them as my survival kit for chaos. And yes, I'm about to hand them to you.

Now, fair warning: This isn't a test. There's no score, no right answer, no gold star at the end. Just a chance to look at yourself—and your own chaos crew—in a way that might feel new, honest, or maybe even a little uncomfortable in the best possible way.

Let's start with the first action—the one I believe is the most important, the one that sets the tone for all the others.

Action #1: Take Responsibility

In other words, own your shit, even when it's on fire. It's so easy to fall into the trap of playing the victim, and believe me, I know. Been there, done that, bought the T-shirt and spilled tequila on it! But when you're the victim, you're giving away your power. The only way to get it back is to grab the damn wheel yourself, even if you're swerving all over the highway. Take ownership for yourself, your actions, and for the choices you've made and for the repercussions of those choices, which is the hard part.

When I came back to Florida, I had a lot of wreckage to clean up—my dad, my best friends, and basically anyone who had been within blast radius of my pain. Pain was the only language I knew at that point. I had questions I didn't know how to answer: *Why am I still carrying this weight? Why do I hate myself so much? Why does anger feel safer than joy?* Deep down, I knew life could be different. But knowing it and living it are two very different things.

It's not taking responsibility to say, "Oh, I reacted that way because you did something that made me mad." I was allowing myself to react, blaming other people. That's not responsibility—that's outsourcing your bullshit. At the end of the day, the only person I can control is me. My reactions, my words, my behavior—whether I explode, implode, or deal with something like a halfway functional adult—that's on me.

And yeah, my childhood? Not exactly Nick at Nite material. I used to stew over how unfair it was that I didn't have a cardigan-wearing, coffee-drinking TV mom who gave pep talks after heartbreak. But no one ever promised me Donna Reed as a mom. That was a fantasy I built—and it was time to stop hating reality for not matching my imaginary reruns.

Instead, I had grandparents who stepped up, a dad who kept me clothed and fed, and the chance to get an education. Did I have to fight harder? Yep. Did I have to get scrappier? Absolutely. But I wasn't abandoned on the streets at eight. I had blessings too, even if they didn't look like the shiny sitcom version I wanted. Resentment was eating me alive and responsibility meant letting it go before it turned me into a permanent rage goblin.

My upbringing isn't what made me. Maybe what happened to me wasn't supposed to happen, but it gave me the tenacity I have today. I wish I could go back and tell myself: Don't be resentful. Don't be angry. Be smart, fight, but take it all in. Be.

Taking responsibility also meant making amends. And let me tell you, apologizing sucks. After a suicide attempt, people treat you like you're broken. They baby you, excuse you, and protect you. Meanwhile, I was drowning in guilt because I knew I had hurt people. So when I started apologizing, a lot of them waved it off: "No, no, you don't need to apologize." But that's bullshit. I did need to. Maybe not for them, but for myself.

Life has a sick sense of humor with its timing. I don't believe in coincidences, so of course the universe decided to mess with me mid-sentence. As I was writing this exact chapter about responsibility, my phone buzzed with a text from my friend Madison. Attached was a photo of a letter I had written her back then, my handwriting shaky, my head a mess, but my heart finally starting to crack open.

It said: *Madison, you are so important in my life; I'm sorry that I hurt you. I'm sorry that I put you through all of this stuff. I want to be a better person for you. I don't want to just be a better person for you though, but for myself, too.*

I need to get my shit together. I need to find out who I am. I need to get my emotional senses back in order and I need to not put you and the people I love through all this hell and torture. It's not fair to you. It's not fair to anyone. And I'm sorry that I'm doing that.

No matter what your current circumstance is, you do have to apologize. Maybe that's the real reason you picked up this book. Maybe that's where people need to take the strength to say, "Okay, I'm not apologizing for you, then. I'm apologizing for myself."

I also apologized to Samantha, who literally saved my life. She found me on the floor, bleeding. She jokes now that it's her permanent trump card: "I saved your life, I can be a bitch." And my answer? "Yes, queen, carry on."

But taking responsibility meant apologizing not just to her, but to so many people in my life, both before and after my suicide attempts, my rage, my quiet descent into chaos disguised as control. I pushed a lot of people out into the freezing storm of my self-hate, convincing myself I didn't deserve their love, their attention, or even their presence in my life.

Repairing my relationship with my dad was hard. But it wasn't hard because he made it hard—it was hard because no matter how many times I apologized, it never felt like enough. I never felt like enough. With every apology, I was still lost, not knowing how to move forward. How anyone could ever forgive me for the hell I had put them through?

When I first started making amends, I wasn't close with my mom's side of the family at all. No bonds with anyone, barely any relationship with my mother. It wasn't until my late twenties that I even began trying to rebuild something with her. I knew I had to try to bridge that gap—it was part of the bigger picture of taking responsibility, facing the wreckage I'd left behind, and owning how my choices affected people.

It's hard. Brutally hard. But responsibility is like spring cleaning for the soul—ugly while you're in it, freeing when it's done. Taking responsibility will break you open. It will force you to look at the mess you've created and decide what you're going to do with it. If you can stop running, if you can take a hard inventory of what's good in your life and what's poisoning it, you give yourself the chance to actually live, not just survive.

Ask yourself: if something in your life feels "bad", is it because you're clinging to it out of habit, or because someone else is actively dumping it on you? If it's you, let that shit go. If it's them, let them go. Either way, the power is yours. That's real responsibility. That's how you take your life back.

Your unhappiness, pain, and heartache don't have to be forever. Take responsibility so you can heal. You are your own gatekeeper to the adventure park that is your life—minus the murderous T-Rexes and those bizarre frilled clown-dinosaurs hiding in car seats.

Life is hard enough when you are trying to heal, and there always seems to be a catch: The moment you start doing the hard work of healing, the world has a way of throwing labels at you. It's not enough that you're dragging yourself out of the wreckage—you're also dodging other people's opinions about how you got there in the first place.

For me, nowhere was louder than in the words people used around suicide: *Selfish. Cowardly.* Spare me. People don't end their lives because they're selfish; they do it because they feel there's no other option left. That doesn't mean you don't apologize for the hurt it caused—but it also doesn't mean you have to swallow the labels people slap on you out of their own anger or fear. Take responsibility, yes. But don't let suicide-shaming pile more bricks on your chest.

And while we're here, let's be real. This isn't just about suicide. Every trauma comes with its own brand of stigma. Addiction? People call you weak. Mental illness? You get labeled "unstable." Abuse survivors? Somehow you're blamed for not leaving sooner. Eating disorders, sexual assault, miscarriages, infertility—the list of ways society finds to point fingers at the wounded is endless. If you've lived through any of that, you know how heavy those labels can feel, how they stick to your skin like tar until you start believing them yourself.

You don't have to accept any of that. You can take responsibility for your healing without taking responsibility for other people's ignorance. You can own your story without owning their judgment. Whatever your trauma looks like, it doesn't make you less worthy of love, forgiveness, or a future.

Taking responsibility means saying, *Yes, I've been through hell. Yes, I've hurt people along the way. And yes, I am still choosing to move forward.* It means facing the weight of what's happened, without letting stigma chain you to it forever.

There's another side to making amends that can't be forgotten, once you start untangling the mess that depression, addiction, or trauma left behind in your wake: Your pain might explain your actions, but it doesn't erase the fallout. You can be drowning and still manage to knock a few people over as you thrash for air. You might have lashed out, ghosted when someone needed you most, or shown up so wrapped in your own storm that you didn't notice theirs. Depression doesn't hand you a "get out of hurting people free" card. It just means the wreckage came from a place you didn't fully control. But wreckage is wreckage—and someone's gotta sweep it up.

So you do the right thing. You own it. You say the words. *I hurt you. I'm sorry.* And then… the silence. Maybe they forgive you. Maybe they don't. Maybe they read your message, roll their eyes, and toss their phone on the couch like, "Too little, too late, Barbie." And here's the kicker—you don't get to be mad about that. People get to keep their resentment. They get to take their sweet time healing. Your apology isn't a magic wand that makes them hug you in slow motion with emotional background music. Sometimes, to them, an apology is just words they weren't ready—or willing—to hear.

That's where you have to check yourself, because your healing can't hang on whether someone else hands you a gold star for effort. You can't stall your own progress waiting for a permission slip to move forward. Whether they take your amends or use it to line the birdcage, you still have to keep walking forward. Keep doing better. Keep becoming the version of yourself who doesn't leave that kind of wreckage in the first place. Their closure is theirs; yours is on you. And if that means you're strutting forward with no applause, fine. Clap for your damn self.

Let's take a quick yet crucial detour and dive into the topic of survivor's guilt. I'll start by saying that time is a slippery thing when you're reading someone else's words. One week ago for me could be two years by the time your eyes meet this page. Time is also cruel when it comes to grief. One week ago, a friend of mine died. One week since he took his own life—brutally, without warning, stealing not just his existence, but a piece of everyone who loved him.

How can I describe the sheer violence with which his death cracked me open? I can't explain his loss or the emotions erupting from my gutted soul, the ones I thought I buried long ago, the ones leaving me raw.

You've stuck with me this far, so you already know that I tried to take my own life. Were they desperate cries for help? Maybe. Were they calculated attempts to end it all? Probably. For reasons I still can't explain, I woke up on the other side each time, furious at my failure.

Imagine the absurdity: You survive, something you so desperately wanted to escape, and the first thing you feel is rage. Not gratitude. Not relief. Just white-hot anger at your inability to even die properly. *What a fucking failure I am.*

Now, I sit here alive, breathing, with a life I love and fight for every single day. And I find myself filled with shame and self-loathing. I think back to those attempts, so naive, so selfish, so devastatingly blind to their inevitable ripple effect. How many lives did I shake to their core in my pursuit of oblivion? How many people did I hurt without realizing? My choices didn't only alter the course of my own life, they rerouted the lives of everyone around me.

At 45 years old, I'm no stranger to death. This is the age where the obituary section starts to include too many familiar names. Car accidents, cancer, overdoses. Heart attacks, organ failure, military service, and yes, suicide.

It never gets easier, no matter how many times you lose someone. Survivor's guilt always sneaks in. Why them? Why not me? What cosmic lottery spared my life and stole theirs? When someone you love ceases to exist, someone who had plans and dreams and a calendar full of untaken vacations, everything about life feels brutal and unrelenting. The real gut punch: His death brought out the worst words someone like me wants to hear. *What a selfish thing to do. A coward's way out. How could he do that to his family?*

The air around these words is thick with judgment and sanctimony, as if the people saying them have never known pain that deep. I stayed quiet as they spoke, my silence mistaken for grief too heavy to bear. In truth, I was holding a scream, one that wanted to defend his actions, not because I believe suicide is the answer, but because I know the kind of desolation that pushes someone to that particular edge.

How do you explain that level of despair to someone who's never come close to it? Other people can't fathom it. They can't understand it and they hate what they can't understand, so they cast blame. It's human nature to assign meaning to the meaningless, to rationalize the irrational. And me?

I sat there, hating them for their ignorance, hating myself for my anger, hating the guilt that always finds a way to wrap its hands around my throat.

I know that guilt isn't all bad. It's a reminder. It keeps me tethered to the reality of my second (and third chances). Guilt reminds me to love everyone who stood by me in my darkest moments, who held my hand when I could barely lift my head. It reminds me to appreciate the sunlight on my face and the people who share their sunsets with me.

I am so grateful for the life I have now. I cherish it deeply. But make no mistake, I fought tooth and nail to claw my way out of the darkness, and some of my demons still cling to me, unwelcome houseguests who refuse to leave. Depression isn't a quick-fix ordeal, no matter what your self-help podcast or Instagram stories might say. It's not a one-time "red pill or blue pill" decision, leaving you magically cured. It's a relentless, grinding workout for your soul, every single day. You build up your tolerance to the pain of existing, and eventually, your inner zombie takes over: Wake up. Plant your feet on the floor. Acknowledge the pain, let it wash over you, and move on. Breathe. Smile. Ignore. Repeat. And repeat. And repeat.

I'm not here to wrap this part of the story up with a pretty, perfect bow. Suicide isn't the answer, and there is help out there, even when it feels like the world has swallowed you whole.

The truth is, no life is untouched by the impact of another. Your footsteps matter. Your voice matters. Your existence matters. While I wrestle with my messy, conflicted emotions over my friend's death, I'm reminded how lucky I am to still be here. And I will wake up tomorrow and continue taking responsibility for my own life. I will plant my feet on the floor and take another step forward, one painful, beautiful breath at a time. And I will repeat.

I won't sugarcoat it: Taking responsibility is hard. It feels unfair. It feels impossible. But it's the only way forward. I know because I'm still here—still fighting, still apologizing, still learning to love the demon in the mirror instead of letting her run my life.

And because we just walked through some heavy shit together—shame, survival, suicide, compartmentalizing, rebuilding—this isn't where I hand you a quiz. This is where I hand you back yourself. These questions aren't something to pass or fail. They're a mirror. A moment. A pause in the hurricane. Use them if you want. Skip them if you're not ready. But if you *are* ready, here's where you start telling yourself the truth.

Self-Reflection: Taking Responsibility (Without Self-Blame)

1. When you strip away everyone else's expectations, opinions, and noise, what version of you is left standing? Not the performer. Not the fixer. Not the survivor. You.
2. What have you been avoiding because it feels too painful, too messy, or too real—and what would happen if you stopped running from it?
3. Where in your life have you handed your power to someone else—and what would reclaiming even 10% of that power look like today, not someday?
4. When you look in the mirror, what part of you do you criticize the most…and what would it sound like to speak to that part the way you'd speak to someone you love?
5. If your pain could talk—not scream, not rage, just speak—what would it quietly ask you to finally acknowledge?
6. What truth have you swallowed for years because it felt easier to keep the peace than to keep yourself?

7. And here's the hardest one: What would taking responsibility look like without blaming yourself for the things people did to you? (Yes, that's a real distinction. And yes, you need it.) Taking responsibility isn't about punishment. It's about reclamation.

It's about stepping back into your own body, your own voice, your own damn life. It's the first step out of the fire. The first step toward yourself. And the first step toward a life you don't have to survive—one you actually get to live.

Boss Barbie Sets Goals (but Still Cries About It)

Ready, Set, Slay

I channeled Big Girl Barbie straight through the stormy, unsettled years of my twenties. My guardian-angel-in-imaginary-doll form nudged me toward the next phase of my life. Her strength became my strength, her wisdom my compass. I was tiptoeing into my thirties, my heart tender, but finally beating in something close to an authentic rhythm again.

The hurricane winds of acute depression and an abusive relationship had lost their roar. They still blew through now and then, but for the first time in years, I could see the sun cutting through the clouds. And that sunlight lit up something I hadn't felt in a long while: Possibility.

I was still working at the mortgage company. On paper, things looked good. The paychecks cleared, the bills got paid, and I could buy more than ramen and clearance-rack wine. But deep down, I knew I was just existing. I had stability, not purpose. And then, in a move that felt straight out of a Greek tragedy, 2008 sucker-punched the mortgage industry. Colleagues were wrecked. Companies folded, but I stayed standing.

From the outside, I was the comeback kid, a scrappy underdog in the third act of a sports movie. Except there was no dramatic soundtrack, no slow-motion montage. There was just me, clocking in at a job I never wanted, pretending I gave a damn about interest rates. To add to the illusion, I had somehow found myself into what appeared to be a healthy relationship. Surprise, surprise, my love life wasn't a dumpster fire! I was about to marry a kind, gentle man. Life was… normal. Almost suspiciously normal. And that's when I realized— if I was ever going to make a break for it, this was my chance.

Finance Barbie was never supposed to be a thing. I fell into it, got stuck in the quicksand, and pretended it was a career. But now? With stability under my feet and no immediate disasters chasing me, I could finally stop surviving long enough to ask myself a crucial question: What the fuck do I actually want to do with my life? What now?

I studied political science in college; international relations had been the dream. I even had an offer from Raytheon that would have stationed me in the Middle East six months out of the year. Somewhere in a parallel universe, I'm probably still there, dodging missiles and living out a rerun of my childhood abroad. But fate, along with my fiancé's very valid plea to avoid war zones, rerouted me. Instead, I got recruited by an English tech company that specialized in photography and video branding for the entertainment industry. They'd just bought an American company and were expanding, fast.

I came in as a contractor, a regional manager. Turns out, I loved it. I was learning on the fly, hustling hard, and actually having fun. But contracting wasn't enough. I wanted permanence. I wanted a real career, one that felt abundant and empowering. So I asked myself, where do I want to be in a year? In two? At first, the answer whispered. Then it shouted: I want to run the U.S. office.

I rolled up my sleeves and got serious. Short-term goals, midpoint goals, end goal. My blueprint wasn't just about the job title—it was about the woman I wanted to become.

Here's the thing about goals: one goal is never just one goal. It's like unwrapping a gift only to find another box inside, and another, and another—until finally, the smallest box reveals a diamond sparkling back at you.

For every goal, I essentially made a vision board, a blueprint for my future self, mapping out my plan for world domination. I'm (mostly) kidding, but that's the kind of main-character energy I embodied. I was calculating, not in a poison apple, evil stepmother kind of way, but in the kind that holds you accountable and drags your ass forward when you want to quit. I wasn't banking on fairy dust or a glitter-covered life coach with wings barging through my window, clipboard in hand, telling me to "manifest harder." I had stepping stones, stubbornness, and a refusal to stay small.

So, I got to work. I studied project management. I memorized HR employment law for all fifty states (because why not traumatize myself.) I learned cameras, contracts, and the tangled mess of internet connections. I turned myself into a one-woman Ops army. And I climbed. Not by leapfrogging people, but by quietly outgrowing my old titles until there was no denying the direction I was heading. Six years later, I was VP of Operations.

Action #2: Set Goals

Remember those six actions I promised you? If you thought "taking responsibility" was brutal, buckle up. Don't panic—this action doesn't just beat you up, it actually drags you somewhere better than you've been, possibly even with a pit-stop for cabernet and Gummy Bears.

Before we get into it, clap for yourself. Yes, out loud. Alone in your living room, clapping like a lunatic. Pretend you're front row at a T-Swift concert, or at least give yourself a slow clap for not completely screwing up yet. Why? Because you did the hard thing: You stared down the demon in the mirror, dead in the eye, called it by name, and didn't even blink. You stopped pointing fingers and said, "Fine, this shitshow is mine to clean up." That deserves applause, even if it's just you and your dog, wondering what the hell is happening.

Now: Action #2. Set some goals, people! Decide what you actually want and stake your claim, like the badass squatter you are. Here's the part no one tells you: Goals aren't just about the shiny prize at the end. They're about who you become while you're clawing, swearing, and occasionally ugly-crying your way toward them.

Some people say I can predict the future. Spoiler alert: I can't. What I *can* do is play mental chess ten moves ahead. My recipe is simple: A splash of logic, a pinch of analysis, and a whole lot of asking, "Okay, if we do this thing, what's the next possible clusterfuck?" That's not negativity. That's survival math. Success isn't just the finish line. It's making sure the ripple effects don't take you down once you get there.

This isn't just self-help woo-woo; it's real life. At work, setting clear goals keeps you sane in the chaos. When you're running a project, goals keep you from just checking boxes and actually force you to think about outcomes. You're not just asking, "Did we launch the system?" You're asking, "Will it still run when the pressure hits? Will the client renew? What three things could go sideways, and how do we plan for them?"

Same thing with negotiating a contract—if you don't set your goal first, you'll get steamrolled. If your goal is, "I need fair terms that protect my team, even if it means conceding on timeline," then you can walk into that room steadily, instead of reacting like a deer in headlights. Goals are your armor in the battlefield of work.

This habit was born out of necessity. In my teens and twenties, I lived like a stray dog, sleeping with one eye open, never letting myself get cornered, always scanning for exits. It wasn't paranoia. It was life insurance. That constant edge, that readiness to adapt, kept me alive long enough to eventually figure out how to thrive.

So, let's cut the Hallmark card bullshit. Your pie-in-the-sky, holy-grail, "someday" goal isn't going to just fall from the heavens wrapped in sparkly paper. There's no fairy godmother, no angel investor of dreams. You've got to drag your ass off the couch and get to work. Sweat through the mess. Fail forward. Show up with mascara streaks and a coffee stain on your shirt. Cry in the car, then walk into the meeting like you own the place anyway—that's Action #2.

And don't let Instagram fool you. Goal-setting isn't mood boards and glitter pens and manifesting by moonlight. Vision-Board Barbie loves her glitter, but she'll also tell you the truth. Success is blood, sweat, and spreadsheets. It's dragging yourself to do the thing even when you'd rather scroll TikTok until your eyeballs bleed. It's trading short-term comfort for long-term satisfaction. And sometimes, it's boring as hell. Nobody posts the real grind, the 2 a.m. "why am I even doing this" spiral, the rejection emails, the half-finished attempts. But that's where goals are forged, in the shitty, unglamorous middle.

Here's the kicker: You deserve the goals you set. Not when you're perfect. Not when life finally stops hurling curveballs. Not when Mercury gets its ass out of retrograde. You deserve them now.

So stop waiting for the universe to deliver your dream life on a silver platter. The universe is busy. Get off your ass. Set the goals. Build the staircase. Walk up it one shaky step at a time. When you get to the top, guess what? There will be another staircase waiting. And another. And another. That's the point. That's growth.

Action #2 is messy, sweaty, relentless, and sometimes thankless. But it's also where the magic sneaks in. Not the fairy-dust kind, the real kind. The kind you earn.

Boss Barbie Finds Her Voice

Every job has its fair share of office politics, but mine felt like a contact sport. At first, I loved my job. It felt supportive, like I had space to grow. One of the CEOs—a brilliant man who remains a mentor to this day—showed me what good leadership could look like. Unfortunately, the bosses between me and him? Their strengths were…not leadership. Or communication. Or anything you'd associate with managing actual humans.

At that time, I was an operator—boots on the ground, managing employees, running projects and reports; on 24/7. My daily uniform was a button-down, pants, and a ponytail. Function over fashion. Recognition didn't come easy in those early days; I often had to push harder and speak louder to make sure my contributions weren't overlooked.The next two bosses? Straight out of the Old Boys Club. The "women should smile pretty, wear pencil skirts, and stay silent in the boardroom" crowd. Mad Men energy without the sharp suits or Don Draper charisma. By far, the worst part of their dinosaur-era worldview was the sexual harassment.

My first boss during those operator days was always polished to perfection, like she had a standing date with a blow dryer and a personal stylist. She'd occasionally "playfully" suggest that I could present myself better. Annoying? Yep. Hostile? Not really.

Don't get me wrong—I wasn't rolling into board meetings with roller coaster grease smeared across my face like war paint. I knew how to summon Boardroom Barbie when I needed her. But let's be real: full glam just wasn't practical in 100-degree Florida heat, surrounded by sweaty, overcooked tourists while I logged my tenth lap around the park. Mascara doesn't stand a chance when you're sweating like a rotisserie chicken in Orlando— there isn't a setting spray on earth strong enough for that shit.

Then came the boss who deserves his own horror movie: Roy Dunne. He'd march into a room, grab your hand like he was trying to crush your bones, and boom out, "Roy Dunne. How you doing?" The kind of guy who wears his first and last name like body armor because his personality has the range of a beige stapler.

Six months in, Roy Dunne called me into his office and hit me with this gem: Women who wear ponytails might as well show up in sweatpants. "No one's going to take you seriously," he said. I stared at him, trying to process whether I was in a bad dream. Was my hair really career sabotage?

But wait, it gets worse, because of course it does. His next lecture: My boobs. Yes, my actual body became his talking point. Loose button-downs apparently weren't loose enough for my "distracting" chest. According to Roy Dunne, ponytail = slob, boobs = slut. Imagine being told, day after day, that your literal existence was unprofessional. And for a while, I believed him. I thought I must be doing something wrong just by walking into the room.

That's the thing about bullies like him. They don't go after the strongest voice in the room. They zero in on the person they think they can chip away at, the one who's newer, younger, still finding her footing. They poke, prod, and humiliate, hoping you'll shrink small enough that they can keep towering over you. His game was power and my silence was the currency he wanted.

We've arrived at the point in time where I introduce you to Boss Barbie. She'd been warming up in the wings, biding her time while I kept doubting myself. But the moment I realized my silence was the only thing feeding men like Roy Dunne, she marched onto the stage. Boss Barbie is assertive, self-possessed, and has zero patience for fragile egos in bad suits. She speaks up to the Roy Dunne's of the world, loud enough that they can't ignore her.

Boss Barbie helped me navigate who I was at work. A lot of women came to the office wearing lipstick and Louboutins and looking fucking gorgeous. Let's be clear, their power was just as real as mine. For some women, their inner goddess got her go-go juice straight from a lipstick tube of *Goddess Mode Merlot* or *Venus in Velvet Red*, and hell yes to that.

For me, choosing a different look didn't mean my brain cells or my worth faded any faster than the color on my lips. Lipstick or no lipstick, your IQ doesn't smear off with your Sephora haul. Boss Barbie taught me that my power wasn't in the shoes I wore or the shade I swiped on—it was in refusing to hand my voice over to someone who hadn't earned it.

I worked in a male-dominated industry, but I refused to stay quiet. I wasn't about to let some dude in an ill-fitting suit and discount cologne decide my worth based on my appearance. Once I found the courage to speak my ideas out loud, lead by example, own my professional choices—good or bad—and take chances without apology, Boss Barbie's mic-drop hit a little louder each time.

That's when I realized: Other people's superficial opinions don't mean shit. It's not the pencil skirt, the lipstick, or the ponytail that defines you. It's the truth you speak, the impact you leave on your team, and the bottom line on your P&L. That's the beauty of Boss Barbie: She reminds me that the haters' labels don't stick unless I let them. She shows up, rolls her eyes at the bullshit, and reminds me that the only thing that matters is my voice and the dent I make in the world.

Fate loves a full-circle moment. Two years later, I earned Roy Dunne's job. Boss Barbie didn't just find her voice—she took the mic and the corner office.

Self-Reflection: What Do You Want to Achieve?

Let's talk about desire—the kind you don't admit out loud because you're afraid someone will laugh, or worse, that you'll fail in front of the people who already expect you to. Here's your moment of truth: What do you actually want? Not what you're supposed to want. Not what your parents, boss, partner, or anxiety gremlin told you is "reasonable." What do you want to build, claim, become?

Most of us spend years playing small because it feels safer than risking disappointment. But safety isn't the same as fulfillment and it sure as shit isn't the same as being alive. Setting goals is an act of rebellion. A middle finger to fear. A declaration that you deserve a life that feels bigger than survival.

Here are the questions that matter, the ones only you can answer:

1. Where are you still choosing smallness because it feels familiar? Be honest. What dream scares you so much that you pretend you don't even want it? Fear is a liar. Call her out.

2. If fear wasn't driving the car, what would you go after? Not "someday," not "when things calm down." Tomorrow. The version of you who isn't scared knows exactly what she wants.

3. What would it actually look like to get out of your own damn way for once? Maybe it's sending the email. Making the call. Setting the boundary. Or saying "fuck it" and taking the first messy step toward the thing you keep daydreaming about.

4. When was the last time you let yourself want something without immediately

shrinking to fit someone else's comfort? Seriously—who told you your desires were negotiable?

5. What version of you shows up when you imagine success and why do you keep telling her to sit quietly in the corner like she's on time-out for being too powerful? Hint: She is not the problem.

6. Who or what is dimming your ambition? Whose voice plays in your head when you start wanting more? Is that voice even yours, or did you inherit someone else's bullshit?

7. Where have you tolerated disrespect or shrunk yourself because speaking up felt too risky? Again, be honest. How many times have you said "it's fine" while your soul was quietly flipping a table?

Here's the truth that people don't tell you: Growth is sneaky as hell. You take one tiny, shaky step, one brave moment you almost talk yourself out of, and suddenly, you're doing things you thought were above your pay grade as a human. One day, you're terrified to speak out in a room full of people and the next, you're running the damn meeting and wondering who the hell this powerful, competent creature even is.

That's how you become the version of yourself you were always meant to be. Not through perfection. Not by being everyone's emotional support raccoon. Through courage. Through trying. Through wanting more and finally having the audacity to say it out loud.

Part 2:
Full Throttle, No Seatbelt

THE COMA YEARS: NOT DEAD, JUST DISASSOCIATING

My Emotional Shutdown Era

For most people, emotional shutdown is a short-lived experience. For me, emotional shutdown was a whole-ass *era.* By my late twenties, I had lost the ability to feel any real emotion of my own. It was as if I had traded my emotional range for a one-size-fits-all mask, playing whatever part was needed depending on who I was around or what needed to be accomplished. Trusting my own feelings seemed alien as a Vulcan learning to cry. In fact, most of the time, I felt like an alien, watching everyone else on Earth with a detached interest, wondering how they all seemed so happy, so content with who they were.

My twenties turned into an intermission, a break I took from any kind of internal connection. I felt like a taxidermied version of myself, glassy-eyed and frozen in place. I wasn't falling apart—

I'd already done that. I was standing in the smoldering wreckage, assessing the damage, muttering, "Huh. Neat."

I floated through my life, drifting even farther away from who I thought I was. I questioned my identity, wondering if my beliefs were anything more than borrowed reflections. What did I want? Did I want anything, at all? Nope. I was a shapeless lump of matter, clocking in and out of life on repeat. I smiled on cue, functioned like a champ, and silently screamed into the void like it was a 9-to-5. And I was always the employee-of-the-month.

Each day was a carbon copy of the day before. I'd wake up and go through the motions, asking that crushing existential question: What's the damn point? What was the purpose of surviving all the shit I'd been through, if this is the result?

If I'd been able to summon any real emotion, it would have been resentment. Resentment that I'd spent so much energy "overcoming" life's hurdles, only to wind up here, like a walking blank slate. "Hoo-fucking-ray," I'd think, rolling my eyes at those cliché motivational quotes about resilience. What doesn't kill you makes you stronger, my ass. If anything, surviving just made me tired—and annoyed at anyone calling me a "survivor" like it was a merit badge I earned in the Scouts for identifying bird species such as the Fluffy-backed tit-babbler, Goatsucker, Andeon cock-of-the-Roc, Penduline Tits , Bushtit, and last but not least, who could forget the Common Shag. Yes, all real birds. You are welcome.

People loved to slap that label on me when they found out I tried to take my own life. "You're such a survivor," they'd say, voices dripping with misplaced inspiration. I'd smile, nod, and let them revel in their Hallmark moment. But the word "survivor" echoed in my head like the shrill screech of the Satanic Nightjar, yep, another real bird.

For me, surviving wasn't heroic. It was a reminder that I'd given up on myself in the worst way possible. I caused pain for so many people. Survivor? More like a coward who didn't have the guts to finish what I'd started. I know what you're thinking: "Yikes, harsh much?" You're right. Harsh was my whole vibe. I was Regina George in sweatpants, but every Burn Book entry was about me.

Looking back, I think my self-loathing is what dulled my emotions in the first place. My body was overloaded by the endless storm of resentment and disgust, and decided to throw on the emergency brake. Full stop. No feelings at all. Better to be numb than to drown in the storm.

The Birth of Vulcan Barbie

Then came the weekend that I binge-watched *Star Trek*. Somehow, in my emotional desert, I found my closest connection to an alien with pointy ears, rocking a bowl haircut and the color mustard like it was a personality trait. That's right. I discovered Captain Spock: half-human, half-Vulcan. Go figure.

In every episode, the crew of the starship Enterprise boldly goes where no one has gone before, then immediately regrets it. Whether they're fighting sentient space clouds or unraveling time-travel paradoxes, it's like a cosmic "hold my beer" contest of disasters. Through it all, there's Spock, the guy with no feelings, stuck in an emotional circus, armed only with logic and his magnificent eyebrows.

It hit me: I was Spock. Here I was, stuck in a world full of overly emotional humans bonding over their collective near-death experiences with aliens that looked like they'd lost a bet with evolution. Meanwhile, I was just trying to get through life in a world I didn't understand.

And so, Vulcan Barbie was born. If Spock could navigate a galaxy of butt-faced aliens and survive the void with a deadpan expression and a sharp tongue, so could I. Vulcan Barbie had no heart, no chaos, just cold logic, passive nihilism, an elite-level collection of dry shampoo and even drier comebacks.

I was all thought, no heart, just like Spock. If he could navigate strange galaxies, day in and day out, so could I. At least, that's what I told myself between episodes. Because let's face it, if you're going to survive an emotional void, you might as well do it with a little flair—and a lot of sarcasm.

When I was Vulcan Barbie, I was a purely logical creature. I got through life with detached reasoning and a growing arsenal of sarcastic commentary. I was an alien in a world of overly emotional humans. Everyone else seemed to be living on some roller coaster of epic emotions while I stood on the ground, wondering why everyone thought this was fun.

But Vulcan Barbie can't stay in space forever. Eventually, reality beams you back down to a planet that's messy, confusing, and full of feelings you thought you'd permanently evicted. That's when the real weird part begins: You're no longer falling apart, but slowly, awkwardly coming back together.

Finding A Way Through the Fog

Here's the thing no one tells you about dissociation: It doesn't always end with some big, cinematic snap-back-to-reality moment. Sometimes you start thawing out before you even realize you've been frozen. Feeling again comes back slowly, awkwardly, like your soul accidentally butt-dialed itself back into existence.

I think of my mid-twenties as my zombie years. I'd lost the ability to feel anything real on my own. Sometimes the sorrow would leak through, bubbling up to the surface, but it only scared the people I loved. I didn't want to wound them more than I already had, so I traded in my emotions for a pre-packaged, easy-to-digest version of myself. Safe. Predictable. Palatable. Underneath, though, I was numb—sinking deeper into the fog.

Numbness is an odd state. The fog gets so thick, you can't see six inches past your nose. There was no instinct, no inner voice guiding me on how to "restart" my life. Hopelessness wasn't even the issue anymore. I wasn't hopeless—that would've required feeling something, anything at all. No, I was just empty. A void. I was a black hole, lost in space. Ironically, wanting to die requires a certain amount of emotional energy. You need to feel pain or despair deeply enough to act on it. I lacked that energy entirely. It wasn't that I wanted to die. I just didn't care either way.

The thing about trauma is that it has no timeline. People talk about theories of grief like it goes in a straight line, like, first you'll feel angry, then you'll accept it, but people move through trauma at their own pace. You can't make a schedule for when you're supposed to start feeling again. You can't force your emotions. They'll return when you're ready. But the thing about emotions is that you don't get to pick and choose which ones come back. You can't feel joy without also feeling pain. I was so used to the numbness, thawing out my frozen heart was like leaping right into the flames of every feeling I've ever had. I went from blank slate to the full-range of human emotion, often at the same time. One minute I was a wreck—full-on, heaving ugly tears—and the next, I was grinning at the sky like the sun itself had been sent just for me. My journey from the fog back to my full self started when I married the wrong man.

Pause. Yes, I know we all have questions. I promise, they'll get answered.

After years of emotional and physical abuse, I found myself feeling hollow inside, stripped of real emotion, left with an emptiness where my heart used to be. Trust was scarce, especially when it came to men, who'd been a source of pain for so long. But then I met Luke, and things with him felt different.

When Luke came into my life, I was still compartmentalizing my personalities. I was still hiding. I kept busy with new hobbies, which were actually excuses to put some distance between myself and the people closest to me. I met Luke at a poker game, a turning point in my life.

Luke was calm and kind. He was gentle, smart, and funny. We never fought. Never. I could lose my shit and he would just sit there and say, "Okay." I knew I was safe with him. Being in that perfectly contained glass globe allowed me to not be afraid. For the first time in my life, I wasn't scared that someone was going to come down the hallway and break into my room. No one was threatening me or pushing me against a wall or hitting me. Here was this great guy, who offered me something precious: unconditional love.

Yet, deep down, I wasn't certain I was truly in love with him, or if I simply clung to the idea of him and the promise of a happy, stable relationship. Numb to my own feelings, how could I possibly give him the love he deserved? I convinced myself that time would heal me, that my feelings would catch up with the life he was offering, and everything would become perfect.

When I was with Luke, I sprinted headfirst into everything like the starter pistol had already gone off. You know how in your twenties, turning 30 feels like the expiration date stamped on your forehead? Well, I was creeping up on 30, panicking like the clock was about to strike midnight and I'd turn into a pumpkin with bad skin and no prospects. My sister and I had even mapped out our whole damn trajectory back when we were teenagers, as if life was some IKEA instruction manual. Graduate college by 22. Married by 25. Baby by 28. Wildly successful CEO by 30. Boom, boom, boom. Neat little bullet points. Easy, right?

I can already hear you groaning and rolling your eyes so hard they're doing backflips. Because of course, life doesn't work like that. It's not a checklist or a straight line; it's a bar fight with no referee. But back then? I didn't know that. I wouldn't figure it out until years later—after my so-called plan had exploded like a cheap firework.

So what did I do instead? I settled. I told myself it was "enough." It wasn't, and I damaged two lives in the process of discovering the truth.

Luke wanted to marry me. I wanted to want the same thing. He came from one of those big Catholic families, you know the vibe: Perfect Northeast aesthetic, everyone in coordinating sweaters and khakis, grinning in a pumpkin patch for the annual Christmas card. That was the culture: Marry young, pop out kids, and call it "happily ever after." Peachy fucking keen.

When Luke asked me to marry him, I said yes. I'd basically scripted the whole proposal anyway, dropping hints like confetti. The truth is, I wanted the life he was offering, but I wasn't ready for the love he had to give me. I was still too tangled in my own mess, still battling demons I hadn't even named yet. Instead of letting him in fully, I sabotaged it, slowly, quietly, almost without realizing what I was doing. I loved him, yes. But I wasn't ready to *be* loved by him, and that's a regret I'll carry like shrapnel lodged in my heart for the rest of my life.

I thought this was the best life I was going to get: Find a guy who doesn't beat you. Find a guy who doesn't scare you. Looking back, I know now that walking down the aisle was a selfish decision. I wasn't ready to be in love with Luke the way he deserved. Luke never pretended to be anything but himself, but I still clung to the hope that time would patch the empty spaces I felt when I thought about how true love was supposed to feel. I wanted to be able to look back at him the same way he looked at me, eyes filled with the promise of forever.

I still felt hollow. There was an empty space where my heart used to be. How could I give Luke the love he deserved when I was barely keeping myself together? I clung to the idea of him, to the promise of a happy marriage, convincing myself that my heart would catch up with the life he was offering. It never did, at least not for more than fleeting moments. I had my own deep wounds. I couldn't love myself fully and that meant I couldn't love Luke fully, either.

Part of me had been right, though. As time passed, I did start to heal. My true self, long buried beneath pain, began to spark back to life, piece by piece. Meanwhile, I kept checking off the boxes the world expected of me: Have a husband. Have a job. Keep a routine. Come home at five. Cook dinner. Check, check, check. Wash, rinse, repeat.

There was no wild, consuming love or fire blazing between us, but there was comfort. There was stability. I finally had space to actually heal from the inside out—and I did. Yet while I was changing, Luke remained exactly the same. In the beginning, his unwavering nature was comforting. He was safe. There were no terrifying arguments, no chaos, no passion-fueled drama, just the epitome of steady companionship. But as my healing continued, I began to want more.

This was the part where I was basically living two lives. On one side, my true self—the one I'd buried under years of pain—was starting to flicker back to life. My spark was coming back. I had passion again, drive, and ambition, all clawing their way to the surface. I wanted the big projects, the promotions, the chance to prove myself. I wanted to go to England, Dubai, everywhere my job could take me, I wanted to actually stretch my wings.

Meanwhile, Luke was…Luke. A wonderful, kind, and gentle man, yes, but completely content with hitting pause at five o'clock, grabbing a video game controller or hitting up the skate park. I tried to pull him into my world, asking him to join me on business trips to Europe, vacations in Vegas. and every time, his answer was no. He didn't want to burn PTO on me, but Phish concerts? Totally worth the vacation days. That's when it hit me: I was climbing and he was perfectly fine staying exactly where he was.

I hoped he would step into the new chapter I was trying to create, but that wasn't what made him happy. As I grew, I found myself drawn to people who stirred something in me that had long been dormant, feelings I couldn't ignore. That's when I knew I couldn't keep living halfway. Our relationship unraveled slowly and I carried the weight of knowing much of the fault was mine.

Luke had been everything he promised to be: Kind, gentle, unwavering in his love. But the life we shared began to splinter, as if we'd been standing on a fault line all along. As it turns out, I was the fraud when we said forever. He stayed true to who he was; I didn't realize there was an entirely different version of me lying comatose inside, waiting to wake up.

I'll never forget standing in the kitchen, both of us crying. Watching Luke's tears fall while mine did too. It broke something in me. I didn't feel guilty for leaving; I felt guilty because it felt like I'd used him. If I could go back, I would whisper to that version of myself: Be gentle. I hadn't plotted some cruel scheme to discard the man I married. I was just lost. And I know now that you can't punish yourself forever for who stays in your life and who doesn't. People show up for a reason, a season, or a lifetime. Luke just wasn't my lifetime.

The hardest truth is that the woman Luke married wasn't the real me. That's where the guilt cut deepest. He never actually met the real me, and sometimes I wonder if he would have even liked her. What I do know is that I couldn't have become who I am today without him. It took me years to release the shame of believing I had ruined part of his life, stolen years he might have given to someone who truly adored him. The reality is, yes, I took a piece of his life, but in return, he gave me back my own.

Return to the Land of the Living

Emerging from an emotional coma isn't some dramatic overnight awakening. It's a slow, sneaky process, one that happens without you even noticing. You think you're floating aimlessly, only to realize you've been walking on solid ground for miles. And surprise, surprise, you've got blisters, and they fucking hurt.

I don't know if I really even found myself until I was 32. Fuck, maybe I still haven't found myself. The hardest lesson I've learned is that 20 years from now, I could still be sitting here saying, "God, if I could just look back and realize that battling depression and trauma is a lifelong journey."

Some people with depression think, "Oh, I'll get on medication, I'll go to therapy, and then, I'll be fine." But depression isn't the fucking flu. You don't just take a Z-pack for five days until it disappears.

Clawing my way back from the depths took way longer than I thought it should. It's not like I had a magic wand or pixie dust that would just make my wish come true. I was lost in the fog for years and years, no compass, no guidebook, no clear pathway out.

That's when I started to panic. Self-doubt crept in. *Was I fucked up beyond repair? Was I already too far gone? Maybe I should just put a 'Do Not Disturb: Under Construction' sign on myself and call it a day. Maybe there's no help for me. Maybe I'm the project that never makes it past the concept phase.*

I piled pressure on myself to feel like a person again, like healing was some quick DIY fix. Spoiler: It wasn't. The changes showed up glacially. Like, so slow I stared at my phone willing one minute to pass, convinced my phone was broken and someone had quietly paused time.

Spending the better part of a decade in an emotionally numb state of mind was a strange, disorienting way to exist, to say the least. I was living in such a thick fog. I couldn't tell where the clouds ended and I began. There was no instinct, intuition, or inner voice to follow out of the fog. I had no idea how to "restart" my life. All I could do was take one step forward, then another, to find my way out.

In that murky in-between, where numbness runs up against those first pinpricks of real feeling, I started finding fragments of myself. Recovering my long-lost emotions was an exercise in patience. I couldn't rush relearning my emotions. All I could do was stay present and receive whatever came my way.

The whole process was like watching a lightbulb come back on, very slowly. You see a flicker. You start to feel, but you don't know what the feeling is. Is it joy? Is it anger? Is it grief? Here's the thing about healing: You can't pour from an empty cup, which is a really fucking esoteric way of saying "Meet your own needs first."

Once I started feeling again, I recognized that certain people in my life were absolute fucking succubus demons. I'm not just talking about shitty boyfriends and disappointing situationships, I'm talking about toxic friends, emotionally draining family members, even projects and assignments that deplete your precious energy.

Hobgoblins, hellions, and soul-sucking ghouls will take every opportunity to bleed you dry. It's crucial to stay centered and protect your peace like it's the last cocktail at happy hour. You have every right to take stock of your life and consider what you want to keep and what to release.

Ideally, the people in your circle should recharge your batteries and fuel your spirit. If being around your so-called friends leaves you drained, it's time to face the truth: Some cuts need to be made. You're allowed—no, obligated—to set boundaries and sever ties with anyone standing in the way of your healing.

That's when "Byyyeee-Bitch Barbie" shows up, waving a hand that's barely holding it together as she drags the dead weight to the curb. No drama, no apologies, just a one-way ticket out of your life.

I put up walls when my mom and her side of the family tried to wedge their way back into my life. I hit pause on a friend who was, frankly, an emotional succubus. She pulled everything into her orbit. Every conversation, every crisis was about her, all the time. She drained more energy than I had to give, so I told her I couldn't stay in her life. I cut myself loose.

If someone is bleeding you dry—emotionally, financially, energetically—they'll keep doing it for as long as you allow it. Parasites don't stop feeding themselves; you have to stop serving the buffet. When something in your life feels heavy or toxic, ask yourself: Is it bad because I'm clutching it like a lifeline? Or is it bad because someone else is inflicting it on me? If you're the one holding on tight to the poison, it's time to unclench your fist. Release it. Release them.

If you're not adding to my life, I'll cut ties. Clean. No drama, no fireworks. I don't wish you ill—I just don't wish you anything at all. Silence can be louder than venom. Sometimes, that's the only way to protect the life you want to live. That's not being heartless, that's self-preservation.

As long as you cling to the negative, you'll stay blind to all of the good that's been right in front of you the whole damn time, your second (and third) chances, your shot at joy, your peace. You deserve better. Always.

Going no-contact isn't always permanent. Sometimes it's just a season, a necessary pause while you tend to your own wounds and emotional needs. That's the beauty of boundaries: They don't burn down bridges; they just close them until you're ready to let someone cross again. Reconciliation is possible. Repair is possible. Sometimes you have to let go of a relationship as it was so it has a chance to become what it *could* be.

It's time for one final moment of appreciation for Vulcan Barbie, Patron Saint of Emotional Detachment. A lot of the people I cut out of my life slammed me for being callous. They criticized me, saying I was a thoughtless shell of myself. Here's the thing: They're not wrong. I had become a shell of myself. I had to get ruthless about healing. And I have no regrets.

There's no roadmap for regrowing emotions. Returning to the land of the living was a messy and chaotic journey. It was like having an awkward conversation between who I once was and who I was about to become. If you're navigating your way home to yourself, here's what you need to know:

1. Take Baby Steps to Feel Anything (Even Cringe-Worthy Joy): It might start with the smallest, silliest things—a song that randomly resonates (Yes, Taylor, I will shake, shake, shake it off), a meme that makes you laugh until you snort, ugly crying every time you see that USAA commercial where the soldier comes home to their dog, or the smug satisfaction that comes from flipping a perfect crepe in the privacy of your own kitchen, where no one can see it but you. Emotions aren't choosy; they'll creep back in through the cracks.

2. Permission to Feel (Even the Messy Stuff): After spending so long blocking your emotions, having all the feels—especially the

hard ones—can be terrifying. But giving yourself permission to be sad, angry, or just plain weird is part of remembering that emotions don't always bite (and even if they do, you'll survive).

3. Rediscovering Old Hobbies (or Inventing New Ones): Going back to hobbies or interests you abandoned in the void can be grounding. Consider knitting scarves for no one in particular or writing haikus about how much you hate the person in the car in front of you during morning traffic. If old flames don't ignite, try new ones, like deciding to master the art of knife throwing in your backyard, as your New Year's resolution— true story.

4. Connecting with People (Even the Butt-Faced Aliens): This is a hard one, so, start small. Try tolerating the annoying pings from a group chat or making awkward eye contact with strangers who want to talk to you in airports. (Oh, why did God curse me with "Resting Disney face?") Every connection, no matter how shallow or meaningful, can remind you that humans are (mostly) worth the effort.

5. Therapy, Therapy, Therapy: Sometimes, you need someone to sit across from you, nodding professionally while you explain how you emotionally identify with Spock in a mustard turtleneck. Therapists are great for that.

6. Giving Yourself Grace (and Maybe Some Sarcasm): No one emerges from emotional numbness as a fully-formed person with a checklist of hopes, dreams, and a Pinterest-worthy vision board. It's okay to feel clumsy, to fail, to question why you're even bothering. A little self-compassion (or at least an occasional laugh at your own expense) goes a long way.

Therefore, henceforth, in conclusion, etcetera, blah, blah, blah…Recovery from the void is less about "fixing" yourself and more about stumbling into new versions of who you're becoming, one tiny, awkward, hilarious, and sometimes tear-stained step at a time.

Find the Target and Throw Like Your Life Depends on It

From Breakdown to Bullseye

The fog was lifting. I was finally emerging from my era of emotional detachment as a version of myself I could begin to recognize. For the first time in years, I was figuring out how to own my choices, even when it hurt.

I tried to kill myself. That wasn't my mom's fault. It wasn't my dad's fault. It wasn't anyone's fault. It was mine. I was young. I was inexperienced. Yes, a lot of bad shit happened, but no one pushed me over the edge. I gave up on myself. I let myself fall.

And yet—the same person who gave up also learned how to rebuild. That became my Aha! Moment: *Don't fucking give up on yourself.* It sounds simple, but it took me another decade to truly absorb it. There was no dramatic thunderclap, no booming voice from the sky saying *You've arrived.* It came slowly, one step at a time, through painful self-awareness and the grit of not quitting.

The truth? I'm still in the middle of that Aha! Moment. Every single day, I remind myself: *Don't give up on yourself.* Those five words aren't soft or inspirational. They're a command. A survival tool. A promise I keep making to myself—and now, to you.

Because I am here. I am better than okay; I am good. Sometimes great, sometimes can't get out to bed, sometimes the best I think I'll ever be. This book isn't written from the wreckage. It's written from the rebuilding. I share these truths not to dwell in the darkness, but to show you there is a way through it or at least to stay strong enough until the light starts to break through.

Setting the target is one thing. Throwing the dart—over and over again—is how you change your life.

Home Improvement Barbie: Demo Day for Bullshit

Allow me to introduce Home Improvement Barbie—fixer of foundations, architect of ambitions, builder of dreams. She's got her shit *almost* together. She knows her power tools, can tile a backsplash like a boss, and she's finally learned not to hang shelves while emotionally unstable or after inviting Bourbon Barbie to "help." (Last time, she cried into the level and everything came out crooked.)

What makes Home Improvement Barbie dangerous—in the best possible way—is that she doesn't lift a hammer until she knows exactly what she's building. She starts with a blueprint. A vision. A well-defined, clearly articulated purpose. Not because she's obsessive—okay, a little—but because of carpentry's first truth: If you just start swinging, you don't get a house. You get a pile of wood and regrets.

The same goes for your actual life. Most of us spend years reacting: Patching holes, plastering cracks, praying the next move is the magic fix. But hope isn't a strategy, and action without intention is just noise. You have to cut through the static if you want to be heard.

So I knelt at the altar of Home Improvement Barbie and made a plan. First: Set intentions. I was already kicking ass at work—the sparks were there, the fire lit. All I had to do was fan the flames.

I'd started at my company as a contractor and fought my way to a permanent role. Then, I set my sights on Director. I was expanding the division, bringing in clients, pushing tech innovations, and yet… my career trajectory was tractionless. Part of that inertia was the résumé people thought I didn't have. Part of it was that I looked younger than I was. Mostly, it was a revolving door of leadership: a carousel of interchangeable suits who never seemed to see me, even as they greenlit my ideas.

As it turns out, if you keep replacing one stale suit with another, you get a hamster wheel of mediocrity. I got raises, sure. Bonuses, sometimes. But not the thing I actually wanted: A seat at the table. So I decided to stop waiting for a chair and build my own.

There were hurdles ahead and predators below, but I refused to be the victim—or the cautionary tale. I would not be defined by the consequences of what happened to me. I chose to control what I could: My voice. I made the brave, bold, possibly disastrous decision to speak up and call out sexual harassment.

When it started, I assumed HR knew. I assumed they'd step in. But the HR rep who saw it didn't report it—because she was a woman being harassed, too. Could I blame her for staying quiet while I was thrown to the wolves? I did, a little. But I also knew she was battling her own demons, maybe protecting her job, maybe dealing with things I couldn't see. What I *could* see—what's burned into my memory—is my boss locking me in his office for three hours. Yes, actually locking the door behind me. Nothing physical happened, but the verbal onslaught was enough: Belittling, woman-hating comments that made my blood boil.

I'm not going to lie—at 17, thanks to my Marine Security Guard "big brothers," I learned a few things about how to make a body disappear. I never thought that particular skill set would come in handy, but at that moment…I was glad I thought twice. Even now, writing about it makes my skin crawl. "Not okay" doesn't even scratch the surface.

I couldn't keep living inside the same vicious, demeaning loop. So I did what Home Improvement Barbie would do: I documented the damage, drew a line, and reinforced the beams. I built my case like a renovation plan—measure twice, cut once. I wrote a detailed, timestamped email with names, dates, and receipts, and sent it straight to the CEO.

There were only two possible outcomes: Real help from the top or a hard, fast exit. Either way, I'd already chosen myself. I had assessed the risk; now I braced for impact—hard hat on, foundation set, ready for whatever came crashing down. And that's where Action #3 comes in.

Action #3: Succeed on Purpose

So, you've saddled up to Action #3 and you're ready to succeed on purpose. Don't freak out. This is where it actually gets good.

Step One: Set the stage for your success. If you're doing the same shit you've always done and expecting something new, you're not manifesting, you're just spinning your wheels in the mud. You can't wish your way into a better future. You have to build momentum. You have to get brutally honest with yourself and ask: *What am I doing on autopilot that isn't working? What no longer serves me? What can I finally let go of?*

I'm not just the inventor of Action #3, I'm also a card-carrying member. For too long, I let life happen to me, like I was just riding shotgun in my own story. But eventually, I grabbed the wheel, slammed the brakes, and whipped a U-turn. It was terrifying. It was liberating. And it was on purpose.

Now, I know that "succeeding on purpose" sounds like both an inspirational poster and a low-key impossibility, but here's the secret: You already know how to do it. Just circle back to Action #2: Plan for every possible outcome. That's exactly what I did after I hit send on that email.

I asked myself, *If I do this, what's the fallout?* Door A: Nothing happens, and I keep suffering in silence. Door B: I get called "difficult," phased out, and shown the exit. Either way, I needed a contingency plan. I checked my savings. I polished my résumé. I started quietly networking. And I took a long, hard look at what I actually wanted next. This wasn't some spaghetti test where I hurled pasta at the wall to see what stuck. I acted with intention. Even if I failed, it was going to be a purposeful failure.

And then, the unexpected occurred: My email was taken seriously. I was flown to the company's UK head office. Sitting across from the CEO, I went full-on brag mode—no humility, no shrinking. I rattled off every initiative I'd led in the past year and a half, complete with documentation and receipts. I wasn't just hoping they'd notice anymore; I made damn sure they couldn't ignore me.

Then came the fireworks. I told the CEO point-blank: "I don't know what's going to happen with my current boss. But give me a chance."

Eight months later, I replaced my boss.

Not overnight. Not by accident. Not because someone felt generous.

For eight months I worked my ass off in the interim role—doing the job without the title, without the pay bump, and without the safety net. Eight months of proving I could do it, do it well, and do it without setting the building on fire. I handled the messes. I made the calls. I carried the responsibility. And when the dust finally settled, I officially landed the role I'd been chasing.

Scary? Yes.

Strategic? Absolutely.

Purposeful? Every second.

But success, like drywall, can be temporary.

About a year into my role, my beloved CEO left.

The one who saw me. The one who trusted me. The one who promoted me because I'd already been doing the job and doing it well.

His replacement was intelligent , self-assured and driven, even if we didn't always agree on strategy or deals. But that's business. Tough nuggets. You don't get a vote on every call confirmation when you're not the one in the corner office.

One of those decisions was the acquisition of a company that was already going under.

On paper, it should've been simple. Straightforward. Clean. A classic "we take the assets, streamline the operations, and move on" situation.

Except for one little wrinkle. As part of the acquisition, we weren't just buying the company—we were also inheriting its owner and CEO.

The plan, allegedly, was for him to serve as the non-operative face of the business. Translation: an overpaid mascot with a title. At least at first. A transitional presence. A slow fade into retirement. He obviously did not understand the definition of "fade". This is how I found myself going zero for two on the shitty boss train.

Enter: the rat-faced, arrogant "non-operative executive". A man who had already driven two businesses into bankruptcy, yet somehow arrived with swagger intact and ego fully inflated.

It took me zero minutes to realize that any universe where this man and I were required to coexist professionally was going to be… impossible. Comically impossible. Like asking a raccoon and a Roomba to share a studio apartment.

He took no time proving I was correct.

First offense: the pet names.

He was apparently incapable of speaking to me without calling me sweetie or honey. Not once. Not ironically. Constantly. As if my job title came with a slice of blueberry pie and permission.

Second offense: our very first real meeting.

We sat down to discuss the acquisition—what the buyout would look like, how the business actually operated, and what shape it was in (spoiler: not great). In what I assume he thought were words of encouragement—or some fossilized form of praise—he told me I'd done "a fine job handling what was big boys' work."

Big boys' work.

Said to the woman who had just spent almost two years doing the job he never managed to do successfully. Twice.

Third offense: day one arrogance.

Less than twenty-four hours after stepping into our office, he announced that he and "his boys" were going to get the company "spinning like a top"—or some other deeply fucked-up euphemism for success that I've mercifully blocked out.

I remember thinking, I'm sorry… didn't you and "your boys" just bankrupt two companies?

But sure. Spin away.

Maybe what happened next was destined, or maybe it was triggered by prolonged stress and a workplace marinated in toxicity—but something lit the fuse on what would soon become a series of life-threatening autoimmune diagnosis. Within weeks I was hospitalized. I asked about taking

Family and Medical Leave and was assured I didn't need to. Reader, I absolutely did.

Just as my health started stabilizing and the content of my newest concerns over "Rat-man" reached their highest levels, the company suddenly decided I was "redundant." So cute, right?

Nope. Not today, Satan.

I refused to be a disposable casualty in someone else's broken system. I refused to sit quietly and let them erase me. I leveraged what I'd built, negotiated hard with the help of close relationships I had made, and walked away on my own terms, with close to six figures in settlement and no non-compete—in other words, a clean exit.

Like Home Improvement Barbie always says: If the foundation's rotten, tear the whole damn house down and build your own.

Real Life Plot Twist: The Fixer-Upper Fiasco

Let me tell you a little story. A cautionary tale, if you will. Once upon a trauma-riddled time, I bought a fixer-upper. A real "has potential" kind of place that I acquired with no budget, no solid plan, and a charmingly awful boyfriend who swore he'd help make it my dream home. You know the type: Big promises, small toolbox, emotional availability of a toaster.

Guess what? He let me down. He broke my heart. And while he was at it, he broke my spirit, too. There I was, standing in a half-demoed house, knee-deep in shattered expectations, broken tiles, and a creeping sense of *what the actual fuck have I done?*

That heartbreak was the best thing that could have happened. Because in the wreckage, I finally saw the truth: I had never actually defined my dream. I'd hoped, I'd wished, I'd daydreamed on Pinterest boards. But I never said, *This is what I want. This is how it looks. This is how I'll know when I've built it.*

I was waiting for someone else to build my vision for me. Spoiler: They didn't. They couldn't. They *shouldn't.*

I picked up the metaphorical hammer and got to work. I became the builder. The bitch with a blueprint. It didn't happen overnight—it never does. But slowly, painfully, beautifully, I started building the life I wanted. I gained a life and house, designed on purpose, for purpose (and obviously, for epic parties that made all parties before them question their ability to party.)

Somewhere along the way, Home Improvement Barbie marched in, ripped out the ratty, out-dated emotional shag carpet, rewired my self-worth, and installed a disco ball in the attic—because healing should *always* come with a dance break.

Life Comes with Blueprints (but You Have to Make Them)

If you want the things you do to mean something—your work, your relationships, your parenting, your Tuesday afternoon—you have to start with the end goal, make a blueprint, and reverse-engineer your dreams. Define it. Declare it. Work your way backward. Wind up exactly where you're supposed to be. Let me show you what this looks like in the wild.

Scenario 1: The Work Spiral

You have a job you hate. Every day feels like chewing glass and pretending to enjoy the flavor. But you stay because...Why? Benefits? Fear? That one manager who pronounces "strategy" like it's a French pastry?

Ask yourself: What result do you really want? Do you want to feel fulfilled? Be more creative? Make more money? Be home before your dog files for abandonment?

Once you name it, you can start hammering out a plan. *I want a job that values my brain and doesn't drain my soul.* Maybe you take a class. Maybe you update your resume. Maybe you make a bold-ass LinkedIn post that says, "Hire me, I'm magic." The *how* will follow your *why.*

Scenario 2: The Friendship Drift

Say you've got a friend—let's call her Messy Melissa—who leaves you feeling depleted every time you're together, like she's an energy-draining Succu-cunt-abus. Still, you keep showing up, out of loyalty or guilt or that weird social contract you signed in 2009.

What do you want out of your friendships? Peace? Laughter? Someone who won't trauma-dump via text at 2 a.m.?

If you want meaningful, reciprocal friendships, you have to stop reacting to the chaos and choose relationships that align with your values. Maybe that means setting boundaries. Maybe it means creating distance. Whatever you decide, stop showing up without a purpose. Friendship is a two-way street, not a glittery toll road where only you pay the emotional fare. Your friends should bring as much sparkle to your life as you do to theirs.

Scenario 3: Relationship Quicksand

You're dating someone and it's...fine. Not bad enough to leave, not good enough to fully invest in. It's Mattwarm soup in a cracked bowl. What do you want from love? Security? Passion? A partner who knows how to emotionally regulate without a TED Talk?

Let's bring Home Improvement Barbie back on stage for an encore. She says, "Commit to the renovation or tear it down, but for the love of grout, don't just sit there, growing mold."

Decide where you want to wind up. Say what you want out loud, even if it scares you—*I want a relationship where I'm seen, heard, and supported.* If your current situationship can't be remodeled to create that reality? You know what to do next, babe. Get out the metaphorical sledgehammer. Smash that foundation and clear the rubble.

Trust me on this one. I've learned to tread into relationship territory very carefully, because when it comes to men? *Whew.* I've made mistakes. Real doozies. Like, full-blown, "What was I smoking and why was it legal?" mistakes. The kind of mistakes that make you question your judgment, your taste, and lead you to wonder whether you should just marry a throw pillow and call it a day.

But here's the thing. Those missteps? That gritty-ass road behind me? They didn't break me. They built me. They sharpened my tools, clarified my standards, and taught me what love *isn't,* so I could finally recognize what love *is.* And a big, non-negotiable part of knowing what love is, comes from knowing how to love myself first.

Now, I'm about to marry the love of my life—a dreamboat of a man who makes me feel safe, seen, and adored, even when I'm an emotional gremlin in sweatpants. And I know, deep in my glittery little soul, that I wouldn't have been ready for him if I hadn't learned how to walk away from what wasn't meant for me.

So, start at the end. Because when you finally get there? It'll feel like home. And baby, you built that.

Action #3: Questions Worth Asking Yourself

Alright, deep breath. Toolbelt on. Bourbon down. Let's get real.

1. Where in your life are you still playing small because it feels safer than going big?

2. What walls need to be knocked down before you can actually build something that feels like home?

3. Are you living on someone else's blueprint or are you brave enough to draw your own?

4. What's one step you could take this week that gets you closer to the life you actually want?

From Gaslight to Wildfire: An Emotional Arson Story

Set My Heart Ablaze (All That's Left Is Ash)

We've hit the cross-streets of heartbreak and humiliation, a true shit show intesection—the corner of *Clusterfuck of Romantic Regrets Avenue* and *Psychological Warfare Boulevard.* Scenic, isn't it? I'll pause the tour here, because nothing says "healing" like a cheap dive bar, a sticky floor, and a bourbon straight up. This moment of questionable coping skills is generously brought to you by toxic men and the unpaid internship otherwise known as "learning the hard way."

I know what you're thinking—whipping out the word "toxic" to describe a guy who broke my heart puts me firmly in the pop-psychology basic bitch side of TikTok. Trust me, in this case, calling him "toxic" isn't watered-down therapy-speak. It's the only word in the English language that so much as hints at his brand of horrific behavior. Dating him was like surviving the spaceship of cosmic fuckdom from *Alien vs. Predator,* only to make a crash-landing into the strung-out arms of *Cocaine Bear.*

"They" like to say time heals all wounds. Sounds nice, right? Whoever *they* are, they've clearly never been gutted by someone who leaves a trail of emotional shrapnel in their wake. There's a canyon of difference between sitting around and hoping you'll feel better and actually deciding to transform.

"They" also say when one door closes, another one opens. But no one tells you what to do when you're stuck in the damn doorway, your spirit crushed, wondering if you should crawl forward or sprint back.

After I left Luke, I naively assumed the transition from one door to the next would be seamless. Instead, divorce dumped me into that liminal, fluorescent-lit hallway of nowhere, the place where you don't yet belong to your past, but you sure as hell don't know your future.

Ending my marriage felt like an epic fucking fail. I'd stockpiled every piece of well-meaning but ultimately useless advice about how to "make it work." Don't rush. Wait until you're older. They said that 30 is the magic number. So I waited until 30 to walk down the aisle—and was divorced by 33. Gold star for effort, right? I thought I did everything "right," but none of it mattered. I was back at square one, alone, starting over, with only guilt and self-loathing to keep me warm at night.

I had no idea how to process the mess, so I did what I knew: I buried myself in work like it was a life raft. Love? Overrated. I was too busy scaling the corporate ladder at warp speed, convincing myself success could fill the crater in my chest.

Then came Garrett.

Garrett was a co-worker from England, the kind of man who wakes something in you you'd forgotten you could even feel. Long-distance, he was flawless: Texts that could have been stolen from a Nicholas Sparks novel, late-night calls dripping with charm, meet-ups in random countries that felt ripped from a movie. In other words: A beautifully wrapped box of nothing.

When he finally moved to America, I thought we were stepping into the next chapter. Instead, I watched him blow his savings on a flashy

Mustang he didn't need and then blink at me like, *Right, so I'll just move in, yeah?*

Within weeks, I realized I wasn't his girlfriend, I was his mother. And I never wanted kids, least of all a grown man-child. Daycare Barbie does *not* do man-babies. So, I ended it. Cue me, dodging the role of "Mommy Dearest: The British Remix."

When the dust of Luke, the disappointment of Garrett, and the wreckage of my own choices piled up, I did what I do best. I threw myself headfirst into work. Love? Overrated. I stapled my heart shut with PowerPoints and convinced myself that if I climbed the corporate ladder fast enough, success might patch the crater in my chest.

And that's when life laughed at my careful plans.

It was September. I was out at a bar, grabbing drinks with a friend before they moved away. Enter Evan: A friend of a mutual friend, 44 years old, a general contractor with his own construction company. One of the most handsome men I'd ever laid eyes on—charming as hell, rich, and not remotely shy about announcing it. Within minutes, he told me he owned two Porsches, whipped out his phone, and scrolled through a highlight reel of cars, watches, planes—you name it.

At first, I rolled my eyes. Who the hell was this guy, peacocking like his life depended on it? But then that little voice in my head piped up—not the "find a provider" voice, but the "maybe this is what driven men look like" voice. After playing sugar mama to my last two love interests, part of me craved the idea of finally being with someone who actually contributed financially, matched my professional drive, and was none too shabby in the looks department. Maybe I was judging too fast. Maybe I should give him a chance.

After a couple more bourbons, Evan let his shiny façade slip. He started asking me real questions about financing and mortgages. Suddenly, the flirting was gone, replaced by an actual conversation. He got my number that night, but instead of sweeping me off my feet, he'd text sporadically, asking random questions about real estate, then ghost me for months like some bizarre work-oriented cat-and-mouse game.

I thought maybe we were becoming friends. I thought I was different. I wasn't some girl he was chasing. I was special. Or so I believed. Guess what? I wasn't special. I was just next in line. Evan was playing the exact same game with every other woman in his orbit.

Eventually, we started dating, but he was always "busy." I planned dates, he canceled at the last minute. We'd grab dinner, he'd leave after an hour because "work called." I thought he was dedicated. I thought he was driven. But it was never about work. It was always about the other women. And how fucking dumb was I to believe him?

Here's the thing: I'm competitive. I love a challenge. And the new me? She came to win. Don't confuse that with something admirable—this isn't the part of me I'm proud of. That same relentless drive that makes me a force at work dragged me headfirst into one of the most consuming, manipulative love/hate disasters of my life. A disaster so twisted it nearly swallowed me whole.

Gaslight Barbie Takes Center Stage

Evan had me pegged from the second we met. He had this twisted sixth sense for vulnerability—like a shark catching the scent of blood—and I was already bleeding out. When he looked across that crowded bar in September, he didn't find me so much as the husk of me: Tired, hollow, a little lost. And like every good predator, he reeled me right in.

The first time I went to his house, I knew I should've run. There was a woman sitting cross-legged in his front yard like a lawn ornament from hell. Her name was Jenna, his ex. According to Evan, she was "fucking psychotic." He killed the lights, whispered that she'd lose it if she knew he was home, especially if she knew I was there. He wasn't wrong. A few years later, I filed a restraining order against her after she tried to run me over with her car. Yes, she literally tried to run me over with her car, barely avoiding a tree. But here's the thing: sure, Jenna was unhinged. But Evan was the one winding the spring. He had a talent for it. He eventually pushed me into my own personal psycho-bitch territory because that's what gaslighting does—it makes you question your sanity until you're screaming at the walls and apologizing to them at the same time.

At that moment in time, Gaslight Barbie made her big-stage debut. She arrived fully formed, with crushing self-doubt, cognitive dissonance, and a sense of identity so splintered it could cut glass. Gaslight Barbie proves some women really can have it all—an untrustworthy, manipulative boyfriend and the erosion of any remaining trust in themselves. And here's the worst-kept secret about Gaslight Barbie: She lives inside all of us.

You may never let her out of the box, but she's there.

Five months in, we were playing golf when Garrett, my former overseas situationship, texted me a work question. Evan didn't even pause. He erupted, called me a "fucking liar," and stormed off the course, leaving me stranded. Never mind his roster of random girls texting him in the middle of the night. Never mind the ones showing up at his house unannounced. Never mind the lies he fed me daily. Later I learned he'd been back together with Jenna all along. The golf course meltdown wasn't about loyalty. It was a scheduling conflict with his other weekend plans, a.k.a. Jenna.

I stopped answering his calls. I ignored his texts. I told myself it was over. I told everyone else I was free. The truth? I was still stuck on him, circling the drain, and I didn't know why. Maybe it was his impossible-to-pin-down nature. Maybe it was my bruised ego—I wasn't used to losing. Or maybe it was something darker I didn't dare say out loud. Maybe what I did to Luke meant I was a bad person. Maybe Evan was my cosmic punishment. Maybe this was all I deserved.

In July, Evan reappeared like nothing had happened, and this time, I answered. He poured sugar in my ear like only he could. My intelligence was "unparalleled." I was "one of the smartest girls" he'd ever met. He wasn't just love-bombing. He was firebombing. And me? I might have been holding the match, but he was the fuel and the flame, dousing me with gasoline and telling me it was exactly what I wanted.

A few months later, he dangled the hook. He was expanding his business from general contractor to developer. He needed my help. That was all it took. He made me feel indispensable. I was done for. Hooked. I sacrificed my social life, stopped seeing friends, and turned my nights into his free consulting sessions—getting him multimillion-dollar loans, setting up the scaffolding for his empire. He never loved me the way I wanted, but he respected my mind, and at the time, that felt almost like enough. I hated it, but I can't lie: a big part of my professional success was fueled by my need to prove myself to Evan.

Evan may have admired my work ethic, but he chipped away at everything else. My crooked teeth. My broken nose. The constant reminder that I wasn't the prettiest or the skinniest, just the smartest. I'd seen the women he followed, the models, the influencers. I didn't look like them, but I thought maybe I could outthink them. Evan fed that belief like a steady drip. Pretty enough to keep around, but my mind was my ticket. He made sure I never forgot that I "didn't bring much to the table," and I responded the only way I knew how—by working harder.

About a year in, I asked the lethal question: "Where are we going?" And then I followed it up with the three magic words: "I love you." Evan laughed in my face. He wasn't "ready for a serious relationship." He was "too busy with work." He'd "get there after this next deal." And I believed him.

For two years, I white-knuckled my way through flimsy promises while he cheated weekly and blamed me for it. If some other girl caught his eye, he'd accuse me of the exact thing he was about to do. If I grabbed a drink with my intramural football team, he'd hiss, "You were out with five different guys, you slut." He could break up with me and tell me he was "starting to fall for me" all in the same breath, just so he could go screw a 24-year-old.

Then, like clockwork, after a month on his own, he'd show up on my doorstep. Not out of love or loyalty—he needed something, and I wanted to be needed. He knew I'd take him back. The cycle restarted. Every time I knew what was coming and clung to the threadbare hope: *Maybe this time will be different. Just this once, don't cheat. Don't stray. Please, don't leave.*

At one point, desperate, I told him about my suicide attempts, as if exposing my deepest wound would make him see me as "The One." Instead, he weaponized it. He brought it up whenever he wanted to sleep with another woman. *Crazy bitch. Are you going to try to kill yourself tonight? You're fucking psycho. I've got to go.*

What he missed—the most important part—was that I stayed alive.

Gaslight Barbie Goes On Defense

Lights up! Cue Gaslight Barbie! Looking back, I can see the pattern so clearly now. It's almost embarrassing how predictable it was—different man, same script. The same wounds, the same triggers, the same twisted logic that told me chaos was proof of love. Evan didn't come out of nowhere. He was just the next chapter of a story I hadn't finished learning from yet. The names changed, but the dynamic didn't. The truth is, people can only do to you what you allow them to do. Back then, I was an open invitation.

During the third year of our relationship, Evan ramped up his manipulation tactics. He didn't just minimize my feelings, call me crazy, and deny he'd ever said that. He took gaslighting to a whole new level. He went into full-on DARVO mode—Deny, Attack, Reverse Victim and Offender.

Case in point: On one of my business trips my meeting got cancelled, so I came home early. I called Evan after my flight landed, the way couples with healthy communication skills check in on a regular basis. I told him that I was leaving the airport and heading over. His response: "You're so controlling. Can't you just give me some space? I don't need to see you every minute of every fucking day. What the fuck is wrong with you? Why do you need to see me? Why are you acting so guilty? Did you do something in New York? You cheating fucking slut!"

Take a wild guess about which one of us slept with someone else that weekend. As Evan elevated his emotional abuse, my anxiety and self-doubt flew into the stratosphere. My crazy had combusted into a five-alarm inferno of doubt and delusion—which is exactly what gaslighting is designed to do.

Staying with a man who cheated and lied, then turned around and called me a cheater and a liar was beyond stressful. Everything Evan said was psychological whiplash at its finest. The result of his systematic distortion of reality? My crazy rose to meet his crazy, reaching a quantum level of dysfunction.

If you want a snapshot of what "quantum-level dysfunction" looked like in practice, here's Exhibit A: At one stage while I was dating Evan, Batshit-Crazy Barbie didn't just poke her head out. She strutted in wearing heels, holding a margarita, and demanding a spotlight.

I'll admit, I've spent years watching other people lose their minds, thinking, *Wow, what a lunatic.* Turns out, I had an unhinged self, living rent-free in my own attic the whole time. Evan, bless his manipulative little heart, opened that door and handed her a microphone. Between the gaslighting, the lies, and the mental gymnastics required to stay sane, my inner chaos finally said, "Tag me in." I'm not proud of everything I did during that era, but let's be real, there was a certain dumb, delicious satisfaction in reclaiming my power, even if it looked a little like vengeance with lipstick on.

One night, after the usual screaming match and discovering he'd ghosted me once again, I planted myself on his brand-new, ostentatious pool furniture, glaring like those lounge chairs had personally stabbed me in the heart. Then a truly scandalous idea slipped in: How glorious would this look at the bottom of his pool?

Sixty minutes later, I'd become an amateur performance artist of passive-aggressive revenge, sending cushions and accent chairs on a perfectly choreographed, slow-motion descent into watery oblivion. Did I feel bad? Not for a second. Did I think about long-term consequences? Please. I rationalized it as a materials test: If the expensive, supposedly waterproof crap survived a weekend underwater, bonus; if it didn't, well, science had spoken. Call it petty, theatrical, or a textbook bad life choice—I call it a masterpiece for the emotionally unstable.

Let's be real though; Batshit-Crazy Barbie is a *terrible* lead actress in the Barbie Cinematic Universe—dramatic, high-maintenance, and way over budget—but she's part of the lineup, whether we like it or not. She's the emotional understudy who shows up when you've been ignored, underestimated, or gaslit one too many times. Sometimes, you've just got to let her have a cameo. Let her toss the patio set into the pool, cry in the bathroom mirror, deliver her award-winning monologue about betrayal, and take her bow. After that, bring in Big Girl Barbie—the one who pays the bills, walks the dogs, and knows how to charm customer service reps into replacing your bad decisions, because who knew freak thunderstorm winds could push furniture that heavy in the pool?

Here's the truth: Everybody has a Batshit-Crazy Barbie somewhere in their emotional attic. She's the one rattling the box, waiting for her cue. Just don't give her the starring role. Let her throw her tantrum, toss the patio set, and cry it out, then put her back in the accessory drawer and let your less homicidal, furniture-wrecking, rational self take charge.

So. Cameo over. Curtain down. The furniture dried. The damage didn't. And the cycle kept spinning. Evan would say he was going to the construction site for the day, but he didn't know that spying was my new side hustle. In my mind, there was nothing wrong with going stealth, cracking his passcode, and reading his texts. I knew which girls he was sleeping with, which ones he was stringing along. The list was long—I was far from the only woman he was leading into the landmine. Evan's infidelity traveled to different cities and crossed state lines. And so would I.

I'd drive for hours to get to their houses, just so I could see his car in their driveways, just so I could prove to myself that I wasn't actually crazy. The conversations that came after were their own brand of chaos. My lines went as follows: "You're not where you said you were, you're in Tampa with that fucking girl again, your fucking car is here, you're fucking cheating on me." His lines were: "You fucking psycho bitch, you have no idea what really happened, I knew you were following me, that's why I'm here, to prove that you are crazy."

The rest of the script unfolded like it always had. We'd break up, we'd give each other the silent treatment, and after a few weeks passed, we'd get back together. Make no mistake, I fully owned my crazy. At this stage in the unraveling of our relationship, feeling unhinged was my go-to emotional state. I had more pressing things on my mind, like the fact that I was deep in my villain origin story.

I was turning into someone I didn't like, someone I didn't want to be. Being in an abusive relationship taught me to be ruthless. It was like all the self-loathing that ran through my veins turned outward. Imagine Kujo after three bottles of wine and serious self-esteem issues. I was the injured dog in the corner. I was hurt and dangerous. I learned how to be cruel with my words. I figured out the most cutting thing I could say, to get the strongest reaction. It was the unfortunate and vicious result of having a quick wit, a sharp tongue, and a broken heart.

Evan was every single one of my failures, standing in front of me, making me ask an embarrassing but very human question. Why wasn't I good enough? If I could just tame this relationship, if I could just make this one thing work, then I would be okay, and everything would have been worth it. Then, my life can be good. I put so much false hope and pressure on a man who was so broken. I didn't realize it until later, but Evan was broken. He's just as fucked up as I was, for different reasons. He'll probably always be broken, because he hasn't tried to heal.

Now I know why I stayed with him for so long. I was punishing myself for hurting Luke. I was punishing myself for hurting my dad, for hurting everyone who loved me. When Evan hurt me, I didn't get angry. I didn't push back. I didn't walk away. I told myself that I deserved it. It might not make sense, but back then, it was the only thing that made sense. If I could get Evan to love me, then I could love me. I didn't realize that chasing after this one thing and trying to be perfect, I chased away everything else in my life that was already perfect.

A One-Way Ticket Out of Stockholm

Evan didn't kidnap me and I wasn't a publishing heiress locked in a vault, but a disturbing portion of that relationship felt like a textbook case-study of Stockholm Syndrome. Hindsight is 20/20, but when I was dating Evan, I was too close to the emotional destruction to have a clear perspective. I was trapped in the wreckage, defending my own captor. I told myself—and anyone else who'd listen—that he'd get better once I helped him build his business, once life calmed down, once I became enough. I outsourced his abuse to excuses: He lost his father, someone must have hurt him first, anything that made sense. He consumed the direction in my life, isolated me from everyone who loved me, and I let him.

By year four, we were deep in our own toxic rinse-and-repeat cycle. There was a six-month stretch where I actually tried to date other people—mostly dead-end dinners and awkward conversations that made me miss eating alone. But then, finally, there was someone who almost felt like *something.* And right on cue, Evan sensed it. He always did.

The moment I started to move on, he'd resurface—sometimes apologetic, sometimes desperate, sometimes so cruel it felt like an art form. Without even trying, he'd dismantle whatever confidence I'd rebuilt, leaving me questioning why I ever thought I deserved better. But no matter how many times I swore I was done, the pull was magnetic. And just like that, I'd be dragged back under.

It's hard to explain that kind of pull when you're buried in it. Everyone else can see what's happening; they can see the cycle you're too blind to break. And later, when you finally crawl out of it, you sit there replaying it all, wondering how you could have been so fucking stupid. But that realization doesn't happen overnight. People say you can't tell someone who's being mentally abused that their relationship is over—they have to feel it for themselves. I agree with that. Pain has to reach a certain volume before you can finally hear it.

The final year was when things crossed a line that couldn't be uncrossed. There was a moment—sudden, violent, and unforgettable—when I saw who he really was, and worse, who I had become by staying. It wasn't just fear I felt; it was humiliation. A kind of bone-deep sadness that comes when you realize you've ended up here again, only this time, it's so much worse.

That night shattered whatever illusions I had left. There was no more defending him, no more pretending this could be fixed, no more dressing abuse up as devotion. The man I'd spent almost 5 years trying to save had proven he was the one I needed saving from. And for the first time, I stopped mistaking survival for love.

That should have been the end. But, of course, it wasn't. A few months later, he called. Said he was unimaginably sorry. Making changes. Finding himself. I told him I was done, that I wanted nothing to do with him. And then, he dropped the ultimate gaslight grenade: "I'm in love with you."

Hearing those words was like being hit by a wave I'd already drowned in. I hated him, but part of me still wanted him to mean it. I wanted that story to have a different ending—to be the one that finally made all the chaos mean something, because if it didn't, then I'd have to face the truth: I stayed in hell hoping it would turn into home. But then came the twist that ripped the last thread of denial—he told me he was already seeing someone else and just needed "a few weeks" to end things with her.

It was almost laughable in its audacity—*I'm in love with you, but please hold while I wrap up my other relationship.* It was the final cruel reminder of how warped my reality had become—and how much I'd allowed it to be warped. That was the true breaking point. Not the violence, not the fear, but the realization that I had made myself small enough to fit inside the cage I let him build.

FINISH HIM: MORTAL KOMBAT BARBIE EDITION

The Three Little Words That Almost Ruined My Life

Alright, readers. Don't exhale quite yet. Unfortunately, we're not done with the dumpster fire. Before we ride off into the land of emotional growth and men who actually deserve you, we have to roll the credits on this particular disaster movie.

Normally, when someone says they're in love with you, it's cause for celebration. Fireworks, confetti cannons, a slow-motion movie montage set to a Taylor Swift ballad. But this was no ordinary love story. This was Evan. And Evan's love always came with a catch, because Evan was all about the catch. He needed time to "end things" with another woman before he could "go all in" with me.

What's embarrassingly horrible is that my first reaction wasn't outrage at him. It was misplaced hatred for her, this poor, unsuspecting new victim who had no idea what kind of shitstorm was headed her way. I hated her. I hated that she was suddenly part of *my* story, the new obstacle between me and the ending that I thought would make everything make sense. She was the woman ruining my narrative, the one who got to be his next redemption arc while I got stuck being the cautionary tale. It took a hot minute, but thankfully—faster than I had with his last round of girlfriends—I managed to stop myself from becoming Psycho Bitch Barbie, claws out, ready to fight for a prize that was never worth winning. I guess practice makes perfect.

It was the same tired line he'd been feeding me for years. My spidey sense was tingling, whispering what my heart didn't want to hear: Evan was never going to change. I mean, come on—he loved me, but he still couldn't commit?

That's when the first truly real cracks appeared. The lights were beginning to flicker, ready to reveal what I'd known all along. What everyone else had known for years, but I hadn't wanted to speak into the universe because once I did, it would all become real. I started pulling away, but I wasn't ready to let go completely. Not yet.

Months after he professed his love, Evan and I were in an off-again moment of our tumultuous on-again, off-again relationship. During my brief foray into singlehood, I met Jason, who I'd end up marrying, but at that moment, I was too caught up in Evan's storm to recognize my true north. I saw Jason as a welcome distraction, an intermission from insanity. Since he had just ended his 18 year marriage, I couldn't think that he actually wanted something serious. I had no idea he would become my future.

Jason was the gentlest kind of miracle. The quiet constant who taught me what it means to be seen without being destroyed. But back then, I was still carrying the aftershocks of years of emotional erosion. I almost lost him, too—not because of Evan, but because I hadn't yet learned to believe in peace. I didn't know what to do with love that didn't hurt. I was still stuck in self-sabotage mode, waiting for the next explosion.

But that's jumping ahead in the story. First, there was the meet-cute—and cute it was! One of my best guy friends who was also friends with Jason, decided to play with fate for the day, knowing we'd both recently escaped romantic purgatory. He organized a casual brunch, invited a few friends, and let the universe do the rest.

The universe provided. The second Jason and I started talking, something just clicked. No games, no drama, just easy conversation and that rare kind of spark that feels both electric and safe. It only took a stack of pancakes, a couple of mimosas, and a few hours of banter for me to realize I hadn't felt that light in years. We spent one hot, dizzying week together before life—and my lingering damage—hit pause.

I was so rattled by Jason's affection—his steady kindness, his eagerness to see me—that it almost felt like a setup. I kept waiting for a camera crew to leap out from behind a curtain and announce I'd been punked. I'd just spent five years in psychological trench warfare, begging a man not to betray me, and suddenly this gorgeous, grounded human was showering me with attention for no apparent reason. It didn't compute and it was absolutely terrifying.

Jason represented everything I didn't trust: Stability, gentleness, the quiet sort of love that doesn't need to hurt to feel real. So, I did what came naturally to someone who didn't yet believe she deserved peace. I ran. I ghosted him, saying I couldn't do "whatever this was." I even used the classic "It's not you, it's me," and it wasn't a lie.

Take a wild guess what happened next. To butcher the poet Robert Frost, two roads diverged in a wood and I chose the one that wasn't even a road. I chose the ditch, the dead-end. I took a sharp turn in the wrong direction, but at least I knew where I was heading. I knew what it would feel like when I hit the ground.

I didn't exactly let Evan back in with a glowing neon sign and an open door. It was more like death by a thousand "just checking in" texts. Calls. Random visits. Local spies reporting back. Before I knew it, his face was lighting up my phone again like a bad habit I couldn't quit.

Letting him back into my life felt shitty and familiar—an exact Venn diagram of what I thought I deserved. I was still living in an echo chamber of self-loathing, the same one that had led me to him in the first place. I'd spent so much time and energy trying to fix his chaos that I'd mistaken it for purpose. Walking away felt impossible.

He told me it would be different this time. That he'd changed. When that didn't work, he even tried the "Okay, let's be friends; you can still help with my work!" line. Yep. He actually had the balls to try and re-up my contract as Work-for-Free Barbie. The audacity was almost impressive.

But this time was different. I didn't believe him. And that was a massive fucking win for Team Me. For the first time, the honest-to-God first time, I didn't feel the need to prove anything. I didn't have to make it work to justify the years of wreckage that came before. Because it *did* mean something. Every mistake, every relapse, every heartbreak—it was a lesson. A road I had to walk to finally reach myself.

And that's when she showed up—Mortal Kombat Barbie. Fierce. Unbothered. Armed with the strength I'd never had and the clarity I'd been too blind to see. She looked me dead in the eye, smirked, and whispered the only words I needed to hear: "Finish him."

I just wish he had stayed finished.

Cut to the next six months: A dizzying blur of ducking Evan, pep-talking myself out of romantic self-impalement, and random run-ins with Jason that kept turning into disgustingly sweet, cinematic moments—tiny previews of what an actual future could look like. Jason was the future—a real one—but how could I risk dragging him into my mess when Evan was still lurking like a bad sequel, playing on an endless loop?

So I stalled. I pressed pause on my heart. In doing so, I almost wrecked the one good thing standing in front of me. Jason moved on. He started seeing someone else, someone who was gorgeous, radiant, and from the outside, exactly what he deserved. And just like that, I had to let him go.

Trigger Warning: Dog Mom Drama

Given my relationship and all the emotional whiplash that came with it, you'd think the universe might've offered me a soft landing. Maybe a bubble bath and a weighted blanket? But no. That cosmic bitch doesn't do breaks. She does plot twists. I wanted breathing room, but instead, I got a multi-level medical crisis that would have made even WebMD Barbie short-circuit.

The year prior, after months of mysterious ailments and unsolved symptoms, I was diagnosed with an autoimmune disorder. Relief came wrapped in dread, because "chronic" isn't a word that ever feels like an answer. My diagnosis wasn't even definitive; it was just another spinning cog in a machine that wouldn't stop breaking down. Immunotherapy loomed on the horizon, and I knew I'd need backup.

So I did what any emotionally unstable dog mom with a Pinterest-level devotion would do: I got my dog, Ripley, certified as an emotional support animal. She was my ride-or-die, my soul tether, my reason for choosing to stay. And if that sounds dramatic, that's because it was. Ripley didn't just keep me company, she saved my life.

If you're not a dog person, I don't know how to explain that kind of connection. Actually, I do. It's called unconditional love. Ripley sat through hours of sterile IV drips beside me, her chin resting on my knee, her tail tapping out the rhythm of reassurance. She didn't need to fix me; she just needed to *be*. Every smudgy nose print on my car window was proof of life—mine and hers.

But Ripley wasn't my only fighter. My other dog, Boozer, lost her leg to cancer and kept running anyway. Every Sunday night, we'd make the drive from Orlando to Tampa for her radiation appointments. I'd blast music and pretend we were on a road trip instead of a slow march through hell. It was me and my girls against the world. Evan, of course, was useless for anything that didn't revolve around himself.

He liked dogs until he realized they took time, attention, and love that couldn't be redirected toward him. Whenever he wanted a weekend together, he'd act like I could just fill a bowl of kibble, make the dogs pinky swear not to binge eat, and disappear. Every so often, he'd drop the classic manipulator's ultimatum: *It's me or the dogs*. As if there was ever a contest.

Then came Christmas. I spent the holiday away, pretending everything was fine, pretending I was fine. When I got home, Ripley looked off: Lethargic, skinny, distant, not herself. Within days, I learned she had stomach cancer. Between Boozer's treatment and my own, I'd missed the signs. I did everything I could, took her to all the best surgeons in the state, prayed to the universe, but all there was silence. A month later, two days before my birthday, Ripley died in my arms.

Being her human was the greatest honor of my life. Losing her wrecked me on a cellular level. She'd been my constant, my caretaker, the quiet heartbeat that steadied me. When she was gone, the silence was unbearable. My guilt became its own kind of disease.

I made a list of reasons why losing her was my fault: One, I wasted time on a man who would never take care of me and that's why she died. Two, I was too busy managing Boozer's care to notice how sick Ripley was and that's why she died. Two and a half, I used her as my emotional life raft until she drowned under the weight of me and that's why she died.

None of it was true, but grief doesn't care about truth. It just wants someone to blame, and I was an easy target. I'd done everything I could—vet visits, surgery, ER runs, all of it— yet it still felt like I'd failed her, like I'd killed my own dog. That's the thing about loss when you're already cracked open: It finds every splintered piece and drives the knife a little deeper.

In a moment of complete vulnerability, I told Evan exactly that—I told him it felt like I'd killed her. I thought maybe, just maybe, he'd hold space for me. Silly me. He stored my confession like ammunition, waiting for the perfect opportunity to pull the trigger.

That moment came during an argument while I was in New York for work. My meeting got canceled, so I called to tell him I'd come home early. He told me not to. My gut already knew why—another woman. When I called him out, he went for blood.

"You're so controlling," he sneered. "You're a selfish bitch. You're a fucking slut. And you killed your dog."

There it was. The kill shot.

It wasn't the years of gaslighting, or the cheating, or the nights I cried myself to sleep next to a man who couldn't be bothered to notice. It was *that* line. The one that turned my grief into a weapon. The one that finally woke me the fuck up.

In that instant, something shifted. The clouds parted. The grayscale of my life exploded into Technicolor, and I saw everything for what it was. I'd spent five years fighting for a version of love that didn't exist. But when he said those words, Mortal Kombat Barbie showed up, ripped off her gloves, and whispered in my ear: "Finish him."

Mortal Kombat Barbie: Activated

After more than half a decade of emotional abuse, Judgment Day arrived. I was cutting Evan out of my life once and for all, but I didn't make that decision alone. Like any well-equipped warrior, I summoned my secret weapon, the ultimate reinforcement. She was fierce. She was fearless. She was Mortal Kombat Barbie.

For years, I'd been trapped in an endless tournament on Earthrealm. Every round, I leg-swept my own self-worth, uppercut my own heart, drained my own damn health bar. I'd been fighting so long just to survive that I forgot there was another ending, one where I didn't die trying.

Mortal Kombat Barbie didn't swoop in to save the day; she handed me the controller and said, *Your turn.* She didn't rescue me. She reminded me how to rescue myself. Tapping into the street-fighting side of my identity was how I reclaimed my power. I had always been strong. Now, I was unstoppable.

I mastered the minigame in between levels, taking on the "Test Your Might" challenge like a true champ. I broke through blocks of wood. I broke through stone, then steel, then ruby. I destroyed diamonds, the hardest gem of all. Winning the minigame was a small victory, but it was my victories, and I was fucking worth the celebration.

Mortal Kombat Barbie hyped me up even when I had nothing left in the tank. Returning to myself wasn't graceful; it was a brawl. But I was reminded of the fighter underneath the scars. I had stamina. I had muscle memory. I'd been here before. The battle between my self-doubt and my self-destructive patterns was raging. I reached my hands out and took hold of my truth, that ultimate prize: I have always been worthy.

Action #4: Be Your Own Hero– Don't Let Yourself Remain a Victim.

The veil was fully lifted. My pink-cloud moment of clarity was fading, and all I could think was, Well, fuck. What now? Suddenly, I had to feel all my feelings and they hurt like hell. Every emotion was an exposed nerve. My sadness could have easily dragged me under. My anger was palpable, a live wire under my skin. I was furious. And, worst of all, I was humiliated.

I was 39 years old, but I might as well have been 19 again. Had he past 20 years taught me fucking nothing? I kept choosing the same archetype of broken, controlling men and calling it love. I kept building altars to people who only came to watch me burn.

My friends did their best. They said all the right things: *He's an asshole. You deserve better. It's not your fault.* And for a while, I let those words comfort me. But one question wouldn't stop echoing in my head: How do I keep letting this happen to me? Asking that question ushered in yet another moment of clarity. It wasn't my fault. But it wasn't anyone else's fault, either.

Sure, karma would handle Evan eventually. The universe has a funny way of collecting its debts. But my controversial hot take? I allowed it. I walked into the fire and stayed there, even when I could've walked away. I didn't protect myself. I wasn't working on myself.

I fell into Evan's poison arms and I stayed there for way too long, because deep down, I believed that it was all I deserved. I was holding onto so much unresolved anger and self-loathing. I didn't love myself, so how could I expect anyone else to? Being with Evan taught me things about myself, things that are hard to admit, but they're true, so I own them.

Evan taught me that I could be cruel. The way he spoke to me—calling me stupid, a slut, a whore—seeped into my bones until I started believing him. I added his words to the already long list of reasons I wasn't worthy of love. And in time, I started using that same language, that same venom, right back at him.

I've always had a sharp tongue, a gift from my dad, who used to read me the dictionary as a bedtime story. With Evan, I weaponized it. I learned how to hit below the belt, how to wound with words. I told myself I was fighting back, but in truth, I was just becoming him. But you can't hurt a sociopath—they don't have the range. The only person I was destroying was me.

Seeing his cruelty reflected in my own behavior was the beginning of my awakening. I didn't like who I'd become. Trauma explained it, but it didn't excuse it.

It took me a long time to shed my thorns, to dull the claws I'd grown for survival. Even after I started dating Jason, I still fought like I was at war. If I got hurt, I went nuclear. Jason could toss a spark, and I'd answer with an atomic bomb. Everything was an overreaction because I was still shadowboxing ghosts, as if every disagreement was a rematch with my past.

When people disappointed me or crossed a line, I didn't just defend myself, I unleashed. Jason would stop mid-argument, stunned, and ask where the hell that level of rage came from. And I didn't have a clean answer. Because when I lashed out, I wasn't responding to him, I was responding to Evan. To Marco. To my parents, my brother. To every person who had cracked off a piece of me over the years.

Evan wasn't the only one who hurt me. I had decades of sorrow, layered like scar tissue. There was a lifetime of small betrayals, disappointments, and emotional landmines that had fused together into one endless fight-or-flight response. My pain had turned me into someone I didn't recognize—a woman who struck first so she wouldn't have to feel the blow.

But Evan wasn't hurting me anymore. Marco wasn't. My family wasn't. No one was. The war was over, but my body and mind hadn't gotten the memo. I had to absorb that truth on a soul-deep level—to accept that the danger had passed—if I ever wanted to stop reliving it. Only then could I begin to rewrite the script that pain had etched into my soul. Only then could I start to heal.

Accepting that truth didn't magically fix me, it just exposed how much work I still had to do. Because even once I understood that no one was hurting me anymore, my reflexes didn't catch up right away. I still braced for impact. I still swung first. The hardest part was realizing that the people who loved me—Jason, my friends, the ones who'd stood by me through it all—weren't my enemies. They didn't deserve to inherit the pain that other people left behind.

I used my pain as a shield, an excuse to lash out before anyone else could hurt me. Deep down, I was terrified. *What if I'm not worthy of their love? What if I really am a terrible person?* But learning to pause before reacting—that was where the healing began. I let their love in, even when it made me uncomfortable, and it taught me to love myself, thorns and all.

That's the real truth about self-love: You don't get to cherry-pick your best traits. You have to love the messy parts, the mean parts, the broken parts too.

I'm still figuring it out. That simmering anger still lives somewhere under my ribs, waiting to flare. But I've learned that staying stuck in it only keeps me in the victim role. And being a victim might make sense for a chapter or two, but you can't build your whole story around it. I wish someone had told me sooner that being the victim keeps you from being the hero. It's a trap, one that looks like protection but feels like paralysis.

Here it is: Action #4. And no, this isn't an invitation to beat yourself up over past mistakes. We all fuck up. We all break things, including ourselves. This action is about accountability, not punishment. It's about sitting in that uncomfortable space long enough to see what keeps breaking, then deciding you're done living on repeat.

My advice for you is this: Find your own clarity. Find your own full-color transformation. Recognizing my reality wasn't an instant cure, but that's not how life works. But it was enough to realize that I had to do something to disrupt my pattern or the rest of my life would just loop like a bad rerun.

I started small. I took care of myself. I tapped into my support network. I got back into therapy. Most of all, I got honest, really honest, about why I kept seeking out people who would ruin me. It wasn't hard to trace. Guilt. Shame. A subconscious craving for punishment. I thought I deserved heartbreak for hurting my father, for lashing out at friends, for marrying Luke and breaking his heart. I had a lifetime of unfinished apologies playing in my head.

My personal life was veering off the rails, but my professional life stayed on lock. Even on my lowest days, I dragged myself out of bed, made it to work, and checked my distress at the door. Maybe it was a subconscious bid for control, for survival. Maybe it was an attempt to protect at least one part of my life. Whatever the reason, my self-destructive tendencies stayed in their own lane. Work became my proof of function. If I could hold it together there, maybe I wasn't as broken as I felt.

Professional progress was a tangible thing. It had metrics and milestones and neat little boxes I could tick off. My achievements were documented, validated, written down for posterity. Success at work made sense. There were rules. If I showed up, put one foot in front of the other, and powered through the checklist, I would end up somewhere better than where I started.

Work was the easy part, if only because my wins were visible. It was the rest of my life that needed a full demolition and rebuild. Emotional growth didn't come with quarterly reviews or a project plan. There was no clear trajectory, no instant feedback, no gold star for surviving another breakdown. I knew healing wasn't linear, but that didn't make it any less frustrating.

Still, I kept moving. Some days it was a crawl, other days a sprint, but I didn't stop. I held onto the belief that eventually, I'd find solid ground. I hoped that one day, the chaos inside me would start to quiet. Because that's the thing about Action #4: You can't just flip a switch and become your own hero overnight. It's not instant relief. It's showing up for yourself again and again, even when the progress feels invisible.

Living with depression and all the chaos of life is an exercise in endurance. It's learning how to keep moving when standing still feels safer. Healing means walking the razor's edge between acceptance and ambition: Honoring where you are while still daring to want more. That's where Action #4 comes in. Letting go of the victim mindset isn't about dismissing your pain; it's about refusing to build your identity around it. Because if you define yourself by your trauma, you leave no room to become anything else.

That's not to say any of that is easy. Living with depression is a lifelong battle, one that people on the outside have trouble understanding. To them, it seems like something you can just "get over." But that's not how it works. Depression is always there, lurking in the background, ready to ruin even the best days. It's a shadow that never fully disappears, no matter how bright things seem on the surface.

I've heard all the inspirational cliches and they make me want to scream. I constantly hear comments that make my blood boil. *Keep smiling. Look for silver linings. Choose joy.* Some people don't say anything at all. They don't need to say anything out loud, they just throw pitying glances my way, implying that it's all in my head, that I'm choosing to feel this way. Well, guess what? They're absolutely right. My depression is in my head. But here's the part people don't understand: My head wants to kill me.

My mind is a battlefield and the enemy isn't something I can see or touch. It's inside me, waging war against survival instincts. So no, being depressed isn't something I can just brush off or power through with a little positivity. Every single day is a fight, whether people see it or not. And the worst part? It's the invisible nature of depression that stops people from understanding just how real—and relentless—it is.

In more than one period during my life, when things got unbearably difficult, that all-too-familiar tightness would settle in my chest, choking off my cries for help. Breathing became an impossible task. Self-hatred and doubt bubbled up like a rising tide, and I knew that my inner demons were coming back home. The world turned black, drained of any color or light. Every emotion—compassion, love, even anger and hate—was stripped away, leaving me numb and hollow, as if I had been cut off from everything that made me feel human.

At one point during my darker days, I found myself deep-diving into research about emotional disorders, like dissociative identity disorder and sociopathy. And yes, I can hear what you're thinking—*talk about escalating quickly, right?* How do you go from having a bad day to wondering if you're a step away from becoming the next Dexter? But that's just it. That's how powerful the mind can be when it's in survival mode.

It doesn't take much for those dark thoughts to snowball. One minute, you're feeling overwhelmed, and the next, you're questioning if you've somehow slipped into a different reality altogether. The mind has an incredible ability to convince us that we're spiraling, that something is deeply wrong, even when we're just trying to cope with the everyday weight of life.

So, be gentle on yourself. Life will keep pushing forward and your body will react. It's chemical; it's not something you can control. There's no such thing as Serotonin Air Jordans. There's no magic button. You can't just pump up and deflate at will, although I'm pretty sure I just landed on my billion dollar invention—If only wishing made it so.

Mortal Kombat Barbie Lands the Last Blow

Over the course of my post-Evan years, I called upon Mortal Kombat Barbie for spiritual guidance and she always delivered. I know, gentleness doesn't exactly scream Mortal Kombat Barbie, but hear me out. Redefining my life took as much heart as it did guts, and that's exactly her sweet spot.

Evan was the gun in my hand. I could've kept pretending that staying was worth it, but that would've been another lie in a life already full of them. There was nothing left to prove, nothing left to win. All he ever offered was chaos disguised as love. So I stayed with Mortal Kombat Barbie, the warrior within me, and started building a new foundation—one that belonged entirely to me.

I'd been knocked down more times than I could count, but I kept getting back up. I brushed off the dirt, straightened my crown, and decided to become the main character in my own damn life. I was done being a bystander. I was done playing sidekick to my self-loathing. I deserved better. I was ready to be the hero who saves herself.

Rediscovering myself meant running full speed toward the woman I'd abandoned. Somewhere in the claustrophobic bubble of Evan's world, I'd lost sight of my own. He pulled me away from the things that gave me life, and that should've been my brightest red flag. I'd been rescuing animals since I was a kid, but during those years, that light went dark. I traded purpose for proximity to someone who thrived on draining mine.

So I went back to what made me *me*. Rescue work. Compassion. Chaos with a cause. It was like coming home to myself after years of exile. Each dog I saved stitched another piece of me back together. I was doing the work—literally and spiritually—and the universe began meeting me halfway. The more love I gave, the more love I became capable of receiving.

That's when Jason came back into my life.

He saw me—*all* of me. And honestly, it terrified me. It would've been so easy to say, "I don't deserve this. I don't deserve him." But instead, I let him in. Even though it scared me. Especially because it scared me. And it was the best decision I ever made.

We built a life together—a good one, a real one—but before I could make space for that kind of love, I had to make space for myself. I had to choose myself first. Once I did, everything else fell into place.

That's not to say it's all sunshine and butterflies. There are still storms, still days when I can barely hold it together. But I've come into my authenticity, and that truth steadies me when I'm too weak to stand. Loving Jason has taught me that asking for help doesn't make me fragile. It makes me human.

Everything I am today, I built from the wreckage, with Jason beside me. In the past six years, we've helped saved hundreds of dogs. We share a home. A full life. I've made friends, helped people, and traveled the world. I let love in. And it changed everything.

Mortal Kombat Barbie didn't just land the last blow. She handed me the controller. And this time, I wasn't fighting for survival. I was playing for peace.

Reflection: Be Your Own Hero

Before you move on, take a deep breath. It's time to reflect. No scorecards. No right answers. Just you, your truth, and maybe the mirror you've been avoiding. Ask yourself:

1. Do you want to be known for what you've survived, or for what you've built after the storm? What part of you still clings to the title of "survivor" because it feels safer than starting over?

2. When was the last time you felt real joy—pure, unfiltered, you-at-your-core joy? What would your life look like if you made space for that feeling every single day, even in small ways?

3. When you feel the darkness rolling in, how do you respond? Do you brace for impact, run away, numb out, or crack a joke to keep from falling apart? What would it look like to face that darkness with curiosity instead of fear?

4. Who are you when you're not fighting? If your identity has always been tied to survival, who might you become once the war inside you ends?

5. Are you still waiting for someone else to save you? What would it take for you to start saving yourself?

6. What parts of your life feel most like "you" and which parts feel like a performance? Where could you trade perfection for peace and self-protection for authenticity?

7. When you look at your scars—physical or emotional—do you see damage or proof of endurance? What story do you want those scars to tell now?

Part 3:
Less WTF, More What Now

WebMD Barbie Skips Medical School

An Abbreviated Version of My Medical History

My early 30s were a free fall; by my late 30s, I made a crash landing, going from emotional chaos to relative calm. After a lifetime of searching, I finally thought I'd found solid ground. But it turns out I was standing on a fault line. Beneath the surface, tectonic plates were shifting, and my life was about to rearrange itself again.

Good health is one of those things you don't really appreciate until it disappears. My health became complicated before I even made my debut on Earth. When my mom was pregnant, she contracted hepatitis from a hospital in India. No one knows exactly how, but the aftermath was clear. She was sick while carrying me, which meant my immune system came pre-damaged.

I was the kid who caught every possible illness, but being sick didn't stop me from doing everything. Some parents keep fragile kids in bubbles; mine handed me a compass and said, "Try not to die." I was the definition of a free-range child long before the term existed. I don't remember much about India, but I remember Zimbabwe—barefoot, sunburned, wild. Picture a tiny blonde blur tearing through the bush, convinced she was part explorer, part chaos gremlin. That was me.

My teen years were split between Florida and Kuwait—two worlds, two versions of myself. In Florida, I lived with my adoptive family, the McCann's. In Kuwait, it was just me and my dad, surrounded by Marines and desert sand. All of this carved my "tough-as-nails tomboy" persona in stone. By fifteen, I was scrimmaging with Marines, breaking bones, and running PT with the Security Guards. I've broken my nose nine times, every finger on both hands at least once, and my tolerance for pain lies somewhere around infinity.

I came equipped with soft teeth, brittle bones, and an iron will. I got hurt a lot, but I learned early that pain didn't have to mean weakness. I wore my bruises like badges. I became the first female pole vaulter at both my high school and my college. When my knees finally gave out, I traded the vault for co-ed football, because clearly, I don't know how to sit still. I was 5'2", 110 pounds, and absolutely feral on the field. Sports weren't just something I did, they were who I was. I was an athlete, through and through.

My body broke a lot, but it always healed. Until one day, it didn't.

Discovering Medical Mysteries with WebMD Barbie

I started getting sick when I was 37. Out of nowhere, my legs would swell, covered in painful, mysterious lumps. I got so sick I ended up in the hospital three times in three months. For the first time, illness didn't just slow me down. It hijacked my life.

Every doctor I saw got the same questions. *How do I fix this? Do I need PT? Surgery? What's the timeline?* I was all "go, go, go," as they told me to slow down. The problem was, no one knew what I was fighting.

It's brutal when your body starts betraying you for no clear reason. I could have decided I was unlucky, but weirdly, I got lucky. On one of my ER visits, I saw the same doctor twice. She suspected something autoimmune and sent me to a specialist. During one particularly bad flare, they did a biopsy.

Finally, I had an answer: Erythema Nodosum. A name I'd never heard but now live with every single day. It's a sneaky autoimmune disorder that hides from bloodwork and only shows up in tissue samples. At the time, it was so rare that I felt like a walking medical exhibit. That's when WebMD Barbie was born.

The diagnosis forced me to make a full-body lifestyle overhaul. Six months of steroids. Forty pounds gained. I was still sick and constantly exhausted. Sports? Gone. Food? Weaponized. I started an elimination diet so restrictive it made cardboard look gourmet—no red meat, no bacon, no joy. Once my system was flushed, I had to re-introduce foods one by one, like some twisted game of culinary roulette. Turns out, I can handle small amounts of red meat, but bacon? Permanently banned. I mourned accordingly.

Eventually, things calmed down—or at least found a rhythm. Over the next few years, I learned to live with Erythema Nodosum, but it was like sharing my body with a landmine. Erythema Nodosum is often a secondary disorder, usually tagging along with something else—sarcoidosis, lupus, or a dozen other mystery illnesses. But no matter how many tests I took, nothing else ever stuck. My symptoms flared, faded, and flared again. Always smoke, never any fire.

I adapted with experimental meds and a revamped lifestyle, rinse and repeat. Years passed and life seemed stable again. I was living with Jason, volunteering with the rescue, feeling almost normal. In 2021, the day before Thanksgiving, I got bitten by a dog. It seemed minor. By the next day, my arm had swollen to the size of a hoof. I'd gone septic.

At the hospital, before surgery, the doctor warned me I might wake up without a hand. That's how bad it was. Thankfully, I kept my hand, but the infection sent my immune system into overdrive. My EN flared with a vengeance. My skin flushed, my legs bruised, my lungs rebelled. I had five doctors trying to piece me together. Nodules formed in my lungs, dropping me to 40% capacity. After ten months of treatments, they suspected sarcoidosis again. Another biopsy, another round of steroids. By the time they got in there, the masses were gone, but the holes they left stayed.

The trauma to my body was staggering. And because EN loves to invite other illnesses to the party, the lab carousel started again. I got tested for everything: Cancer, autoimmune overlaps, mystery syndromes. Meanwhile, real life didn't stop. I missed seven weeks of work during one of the busiest times of the year, with hundreds of employees depending on me, and I was terrified of being seen as weak.

To their credit, the company and my boss stood by me, supporting my return. But my world kept shrinking. Pain was constant. Stress was relentless. I couldn't run. I couldn't do yoga. My diet was a chore. My body became a cage. My blood pressure spiked. My energy crashed. Exhaustion became my new normal. Everyone told me to be patient, but patience doesn't cure pain.

During all this, I started developing painful rashes on my face and upper body. One doctor called it rosacea, but I knew better. Then came another round of lupus tests—negative, again. The rashes got angrier, more aggressive. A year later, a knee surgery triggered the perfect storm: An erythema nodosum flare mixed with the rash. My body was exhausted and running out of fight. My skin would turn beet red, hot to the touch, and erupt in swelling faster than you could blink.

The flares kept coming for seven straight months. One moment fine, the next dizzy, nauseated, and red enough to be Elmo's stunt double. Once, I passed out at a stop sign and woke up in a parking lot, my car miraculously unscathed. But after that, I became terrified to drive, because how do you fight what you can't predict?

The attacks came closer together: every three weeks, then every two, then every other day. I collected specialists like trophies—immunologists, endocrinologists, hematologists, rheumatologists. All of the *-ologists*. None of them had any answers. Just more steroids and sympathetic shrugs.

Meanwhile, the pain dug in. My joints throbbed. My bones ached. If I so much as nicked myself, infection spread like wildfire. Over the past few years, I've had two back procedures and six surgeries, including a microvascular decompression (MVD) on my brain for trigeminal neuralgia—known as the "suicide disease," and for good reason.

Trigeminal neuralgia attacks the nerve responsible for facial sensation with lightning-bolt pain so intense it can literally drop you to your knees. It's triggered by a breeze, a sip of coffee, even a smile. It's said to be among the worst pains known to medicine. My MVD surgery helped, but it hasn't fully cured the disease. I still deal with flare-ups. I'm clinging to hope that the symptoms fade as my body continues healing. The alternative procedure—dulling the nerve entirely—would leave the left side of my skull permanently numb or even with potential partial paralysis. Tempting, right? A pain-free existence where you also can't feel your own cheek? Hard pass—for now.

I've been a patient at The Mayo Clinic for several months, where I recently added fibromyalgia to my ever-expanding list of diagnoses, because apparently, I needed a sequel. Mayo's team believes my extreme flushing and flare-ups are caused by a rare neurological misfire, where my central nervous system tells my blood vessels to dilate for no reason at all, turning me into a full-body inferno of redness, heat, and chaos. Literally a Hot Mess.

So here I am: Still standing, still flaring, still figuring it out. WebMD Barbie's Medical Mystery Tour continues, but she's learned to keep receipts, advocate hard, and laugh through the madness. Sometimes, the only thing more unpredictable than the body is the journey it drags you on.

While I like to think I'm unbreakable, the truth is, I'm not. I don't want to be seen as fragile, but for the first time in my life, I can admit that maybe I am. Some days, the pain feels endless. I don't know what's waiting around the next corner—whether it's a cure, another diagnosis, or another round of "we're not sure." It would be easy to surrender, to drown in the pills and exhaustion and call it rest. But I've done that before and I refuse to do it again.

It's hard to keep showing up when my body keeps shutting down. It's hard to let people in when independence used to be my armor. I still struggle to ask for help, but I'm learning. I'm learning to lean on the people I love and to be gentler with myself than I've ever been. This chapter of my life might never have a tidy ending, but maybe that's the point. Maybe healing isn't about being unbreakable, it's about learning how to bend without breaking.

If all else fails, WebMD Barbie will still be here, armed with a heating pad, a dark sense of humor, and enough prescription bottles to qualify as modern art. Because if I can't cure it, I might as well make it entertaining.

The Art of Staying Upright When Life Body-Slams You

Being sick sucks. It sucks hard. Sometimes, WebMD Barbie just doesn't cut it, which is when her twin sister, Bright Side Barbie, steps up and takes over. Thank fucking God for Bright Side Barbie. Ever since my body pulled a major "fuck you plot twist" and developed an autoimmune disorder, every day has been a game of roulette: Will I wake up feeling like a semi-functional human or a couch-bound puddle of "Why Me?" The pain and symptoms are always there, like an uninvited houseguest who raids your fridge and never leaves, but I've learned to carry it, because what else can you do?

I wake up every day in some sort of pain, but I have to choose to put my positive panties on and believe that I can get through it. If I started every morning expecting disaster, I'd never even make it out the door.

I don't want to just exist. I want to *live.* No one's coming to rescue me—this is a self-rescue mission. If you can't inspire yourself, how can you expect anyone else to show up for you? If you want to keep your fire burning, you have to be your own spark. Remember, you have to be your own hero.

Some mornings, I pop out of bed feeling like I've got this "adulting" thing under control. Other mornings, I have to bribe myself out from under the covers with promises of coffee and cake pops. Most days, my motivation is the feeling of one of my dogs, Little Bird, pulling the blankets off because we're late for his morning face smooches. My rescue dogs are my joy, the reason I keep showing up. They rely on me, and even when rescue life breaks my heart, they're the glue that holds me together.

My dogs are like those chaotic college roommates you couldn't live without—but sometimes wish you could evict. They throw ragers at 6 a.m., barking at ghosts only they can see. They demand gourmet meals at exact times (or the Yelp reviews start flying), and if I'm five minutes late, they act like I've left them to forage for berries in the wild. Just when I think I've earned their approval, one of them "leaves me a surprise" on the floor, because nothing says love like a passive-aggressive poop note.

But here's the thing about my furry freeloaders: They're the ones who make me laugh when I'm sobbing, who curl up beside me when the world's too heavy, and remind me that unconditional love doesn't require perfection, without saying a single word. They're the worst roommates I'll ever have and somehow the only ones I'd sign a lifetime lease with—piss puddles, chewed shoes, and all.

My support squad also includes my now husband, the calm to my chaos, the man who cheers me on whether I'm plotting world domination or crying on the bathroom floor because one of the dogs just peed on my last clean blanket. Honestly, he deserves hazard pay and a lifetime achievement award for surviving me with his sense of humor intact.

I've reached "platinum member" status at Quest Diagnostics. The phlebotomists greet me by name, and I'm fairly certain my veins have their own VIP punch card. Every week it's another round of tests, needles, and the same polite lie: "We're still waiting on results." I try to frame it as progress—baby steps forward—but sometimes, it feels more like spinning my wheels in a mud pit of symptoms and side effects. While everyone's still nodding toward fibromyalgia as the asshole behind the curtain, no one's exactly sending it a cease-and-desist. There are days I want to scream, "Can someone please just find the damn problem?" and others when I'm convinced the light at the end of the tunnel is just a freight train picking up speed.

And you know what? That's okay. It's okay to feel like absolute garbage sometimes, to let the weight of it all flatten you for a minute. The trick is not *staying* there. On those days, Bright Side Barbie steps aside and Bourbon Barbie slides in with a stiff drink and full permission to ugly-cry. Sometimes survival isn't pretty—it's a one-woman pity party followed by a pep talk in the mirror and a to-do list for the morning.

Let's not sugarcoat it: Juggling a full-time job, wedding planning for over a year (Hallelujah, that's over!), six dogs (yes, six), and working with a rescue, all while living in a body that feels like a malfunctioning science fair project, is exhausting. I screw up daily. I draw boundaries and bulldoze them hours later. I say yes when I should say "not even if you paid me," because I hate letting anyone down. I live on caffeine, adrenaline, and pure spite. But I keep going, because the alternative is quitting, and that sucks harder than any bad day I've had.

I don't need pity. Concern is kind; condescension can take a seat. I'm not fragile—well, at least my fortitude isn't. I'm figuring it out, messy, complicated, stubborn as hell, and still standing.

If your life feels like a blender without a lid, here's my advice: Find your version of Bright Side Barbie. Maybe she's your dog, your person, your playlists, or your secret midnight ice cream ritual. Whatever keeps you tethered to yourself, hold on to it.

Life isn't about being unbreakable. It's about learning to reassemble yourself every time you shatter. Some days you'll be steel; other days, wet tissue paper. Both count. Both are human. Cry if you need to. Fuck it, scream if you must, rest when you can, but keep going— one messy, imperfect, glorious step at a time.

Build-A-Bear and the Seven Stages of Psychological Collapse

The philosophy above will serve you well. It did not prepare me for Build a Bear. There are bad days, and then there are Build-A-Fucking-Bear days.

Let me paint the tragic tapestry. Picture it: I'm unexpectedly roped into Babysitter Barbie duty because my now-husband had to work, and someone (hi, it me) had to make sure his then-9-year-old daughter didn't summon the four horsemen of boredom. I was having what I'd clinically classify as a "Too Much" day. You know the kind—when the universe hands you a molotov cocktail of chaos, sprinkles in a dash of hangover, douses it in work emails, and then lights it all on fire with your estrogen.

All I wanted—*all I wanted*—was to pull the blinds, climb into my bathtub, and let the rest of the world devour itself. But no. Instead, I had a 9-year-old gremlin with ADHD doing a full-court press conference to go to Build-A-Bear. She'd been lobbying harder than a pharma rep on Capitol Hill. And like the tired, broken shell of a woman I was, I cracked.

"Fine," I muttered. "How bad can it be?"

I figured I could toss my child and credit card at the first employee I saw and then go sit in the food court, talk myself off a ledge, and have a quiet moment with my emotional support flask—the glittery gold one with a cartoon llama and the words "No Drama Llama" on it. (Oh, the irony.)

But no.

Enter: Our assigned "Bear Builder," a teen-age boy who looked like the genetically inbred lovechild of Beavis and Butthead. Let's call him Butthead Jr., because he had the facial expressions of a confused potato and the energy of a sleep-deprived squirrel on Monster Energy. His job? To "guide us through the magic of creating our very own special friend."

I turned to leave, already unzipping my purse to make sweet, flask-y love to Angel's Envy—my preferred bourbon deity, when I heard it.

"Heyyy, where are you headed, *mom*? You're not gonna make a dream bear too?"

I spun around like a villain in a telenovela. "What did you say?"

"Oh yeah!" he said with the type of grin that makes you understand why certain species eat their young. "Every family member gets to build their very own custom bear! It's bonding!"

Bonding? BUILD-A-FUCKING-BEAR BARBIE DID *NOT* SHOW UP TO PLAY TODAY, CHAD.

In my head, I was already slumped on a mall bench with Crash-and-Burn Barbie and Mental-Breakdown Barbie, watching the world burn while Chug-a-Lug Barbie popped up yelling, "Hold my beer, bitches!"

But no. My little gremlin turned and looked at me with those big hopeful eyes—because of course she did—and suddenly, I'm elbows deep in faux fur and polyester emotions.

If you've never been to Build-A-Bear, let me explain the process. There are stations. So. Many. Fucking. Stations.

You don't just stuff a bear. No, no, no. That would be logical. First you pick your "skin" (creepy), then you pick your stuffing level (Floppy? Firm? Existentially empty inside?) and then they make you choose a heart. A tiny fucking plastic heart that you have to kiss, spin around, rub on your head for smarts, and jump up and down while shouting what you want your bear to be when it grows up. All while Butthead Jr. narrated our adventure like some cracked-out cruise director from the S.S. Insanity. I wish I was kidding.

Just when I thought I was free—when I had a half-stuffed bear that looked like it moonlighted as a voodoo doll for the clinically unhinged—I saw the Accessory Wall and promptly blacked out for a second.

There were shirts. Pants. Hoodies. Shoes. Fucking socks. For a stuffed bear. There were braces—real, plastic, orthodontist-issued braces for these things. Hair extensions. Tiny underpants. Slap bracelets. Friendship necklaces. I didn't need accessories—I needed a 72-hour hold and a Thorazine drip.

By the time we got to the register, my kid's bear looked like the bastard lovechild of Cardi B and a Lisa Frank folder. Mine looked like a rejected Squishmallow someone found in the sewer. But the final insult? The cherry on top of my psychological sundae?

"What would you like to name your bear?" Butthead Jr. cooed, grinning like a Labrador that just farted.

Something inside me snapped. I don't know if it was the hangover, the overstimulation, or the soul-crushing realization that I had just spent $78 to make a plush STD.

Something about being forced to name my emotional support plushie while that sentient jar of mayonnaise behind the counter grinned at me like he just cured cancer made me want to staple my own eyes shut. It sent me spiraling into the five stages of grief, all at once, with a side helping of homicidal rage.

In my mind, I prayed: "Oh ye mighty Gods of Glitter, petty vengeance, and Half-Assed Customer Service, bless me with the unholy power to Care Bear Stare this potato-headed son of a bitch into an eternal abyss of hold music, 404 errors and a never-ending line of Karens."

And oh, they came.

My dream squad materialized—Grumpy Bear with a leather jacket and a switchblade comb. Cheer Bear rocking combat boots and a brass knuckle smiley face. Tenderheart Bear covered in tattoos, looking all bad ass and shit, lighting a cigarette off the flaming rage in my eyes.

Shank-a-Bitch Barbie stood next to them, twirling her butterfly knife. Mortal Kombat Barbie cracked her knuckles. Because of course, they were here too.

We were locked. Loaded. Care Bear Stare: Meltdown Mode went in full effect. The Care Bears didn't come to cuddle. They came to kill, bitches.

I looked him directly in his pimple-framed beady eyes and said, "My bear? What's my bear's name you ask? This one's named Snuggles the Destroyer, my emotional support ho. Print the birth certificate and step away from the counter before I call in Hug-a-Lot Bear to cave your chest in with overly aggressive love and squeezes."

Was I proud of my behavior? It wasn't exactly my finest moment or the best example for the small human next to me, but we walked out victorious, me clutching my trauma doll like a badge of survival, my kid beaming with her bougie bear, and Butthead Jr. still blinking in confusion.

Never underestimate the emotional warfare of Build-A-Bear. And never, ever leave your flask at home.

Mall Madness: The Rise of Snuggles the Destroyer

For most people, the chaos would have stopped in the parking lot. But me? I'm not normal, so of course it followed me home…and straight into my dreams. I'd say I'm charmingly unhinged, with a flair for dramatics and questionable mall behavior, but in an adorable kind of way, like a raccoon in a tiara holding a grudge.

That night, somewhere between bourbon shot number three and falling asleep on the couch, scrolling dog rescue Facebook reels, the dream began.

The mall was dark. Too dark. Not in a "we're closed" way, but in a "something wicked this way comes" way. Fluorescent lights flickered overhead like they were powered by pure spite. The scent of stale Auntie Anne's pretzels wafted through the air, mingled with the faint static of distant mall music—a distorted remix of *Barbie Girl* that sounded...ominous.

I looked down. I wasn't wearing my pajamas anymore. Nope. I was in full combat gear.

Camouflage miniskirt. Combat boots. A rhinestone flask strapped to my thigh. I was Mall Rambo Barbie, and I was holding a grudge.

From the shadows, my Build-A-Bear emerged. But she was no longer the limp-limbed, half-stuffed mess from earlier. She was 3 feet tall, glowing slightly, her eyes lit up like LEDs, wearing a studded leather vest and wielding a bubble gun filled with boiling hot glitter.

"It's time," she said, in a voice like Kristen Wiig possessed by vengeance. "We ride at dawn."

Behind her, the Barbie Squad assembled: Shank-a-Bitch Barbie had traded her stilettos for steel-toed combat boots and she was sharpening her acrylics on a whetstone. Mortal Kombat Barbie flexed, crackling her knuckles with repressed rage. Bourbon Barbie took a swig and muttered, "I've been waiting for this moment since Wet Seal closed down." And in the back, Crash-and-Burn Barbie was strapping explosives made from expired Bath & Body Works lotions to a mini drone named Karen.

We stormed Build-A-Bear like it was the damn Bastille. Escalator? No. We zip-lined down from the food court, landing in front of the store in a blaze of sequins and deeply repressed childhood trauma.

Inside stood Butthead Jr., evolved into his final Pokémon form: Manager Chad Supreme. He wore a headset, cargo shorts, and a lanyard, heavy with corporate indifference.

"Welcome back to Build-A-Bear, do you have a rewards acc—"

BOOM.

Snuggles the Destroyer drop-kicked the counter. Stuffing flew like confetti. A pack of unstuffed bears fell from the ceiling like haunted parade floats.

"You will *never* make me kiss a plastic heart again, Chad!" I screamed.

He stumbled back, tripping over a bin of bear-sized sunglasses. That's when I called it.

"Care Bear Squad—STARE MODE: ACTIVATED."

A blinding beam of rainbow laser vengeance shot out from the bellies of the squad—Grumpy Bear with his brass knuckles, Cheer Bear with a chainsaw guitar, Tenderheart in war paint and Timberlands. Hug-a-Lot Bear? He just Hulk-smashed through the back wall like the Kool-Aid Man with a superiority complex.

I leaned close and whispered, "You activated my inner sparkle assassin, Chad. Big mistake."

Snuggles the Destroyer launched herself through the air in a majestic, slow-motion front flip, glitter streaming behind her like the tail of an unhinged comet. She landed on Chad's chest, looked him dead in the eyes, and whispered, "This one's for the moms."

Chad exploded into a poof of Axe body spray and Hot Topic coupons. Silence fell. The mission was complete.

We stood among the wreckage—loose stuffing and shattered tiaras on the floor, mall security passed out behind the Dippin' Dots cart. We had avenged every overpriced accessory, every forced naming ceremony, every "Do you want to add a sound chip for $7.99?"

Snuggles turned to me, gave a solemn nod, and said, "Let's go, Mama. Claire's awaits."

And then I woke up. Sticky from bourbon sweat, glitter in my hair, the bear sitting quietly on the shelf, looking smug. Somewhere deep in her tiny stitched heart, she knew what we'd done.

She still sits there, by the way, on a shelf in my office. Snuggles the Destroyer. Watcher. Witness to my mind numbing zoom calls. Unbothered. Ready for war. And occasionally, I swear she winks.

Moral of the story?

Yeah. I had a meltdown in a mall. I named a bear Snuggles the Destroyer. I fantasized about rainbow-blasting a teenager named Chad into the seventh circle of retail hell. I drank bourbon out of a llama flask like it was communion. And honestly? I'd do it all again.

Because here's the thing: We all have those days. The unhinged, full-systems-overload, "why is this bear wearing braces?" kind of days. Days where your patience is thinner than Build-A-Bear's corporate soul and all you want is five goddamn minutes of peace.

But those moments—those gloriously messy, mortifying, meltdown moments? They don't make you a bad person. They make you *a person.* You can feel resentment and still be loving. You can lose your shit and still be worthy of grace. Especially from yourself.

So if you've ever found yourself crying in a food court, plotting plushie-fueled vengeance, or just wondering how the hell life got so extra, let me say this: You're not broken. You're just a work in progress.

The world keeps spinning. The kid still loves you. The bear still sits on your shelf. No matter how chaotic the day gets, you can always rebuild—you don't even need stuffing or a sound chip. Just a little forgiveness, a deep breath, and maybe a backup flask. And if nothing else, you'll have one hell of a story.

Be like Bird: Life Lessons from a Fluffy Narcissist

Let's press pause on my regularly scheduled disaster programming so I can tell you about Bird, a dog whose story is heartbreakingly beautiful, hilariously unexpected, and profoundly inspiring. Bird came into my life because I have "sucker" tattooed on my forehead in big, bold, neon letters. He was just two months old, living on the streets of the Bahamas, when he was attacked by a gang of street dogs. His spine was severed, leaving his back legs paralyzed. By some miracle—or sheer force of will—he survived for a month before being rescued, but not without damage. One of his back legs was crushed, and the other was broken at the femur.

Medical care for dogs in the Bahamas is minimal at best, especially for extreme cases like Bird's. The rescue that found him was fighting for his life, because they could see something in him, something no one else seemed to notice. They saw his spark, his tenacity, his incredible personality, and they just couldn't give up. They sent out countless pleas for help, desperate for someone who could give Bird the second chance he deserved. That's when the rescue I work with came into the picture. Bird left the Bahamas and made it to the United States, and my life has been irrevocably changed ever since.

Here's the part they probably should've warned me about—because if they had, I would've run screaming into the night. Bird can't pee on his own. Nope, that's right. I had to catheterize him three times a day to empty his bladder for the first few months, before his body learned to do it out of reflex. I'm on constant alert for frequent urinary tract infections, all while trying to manage what can only be described as a *poop-apocolypse*. And let me tell you—as someone with a nose that can detect a dirty diaper from five miles away, along with a borderline obsessive need to keep the floors spotless, this situation is pure torture. Yet I love Bird more than anything. He's the light of my life, the furball of joy that keeps me going when everything else feels impossible.

Bird's original name was *Ucillino*—a beautiful, poetic name that means "Little Bird" in Spanish. It was given to him by Dora, the woman who runs the Nassau-based rescue that never gave up on him. She named him this because she hoped one day he'd be healed enough to spread his wings and fly again. When Dora spoke his name, it was as if the words themselves were imbued with magic. His name was a testament to his spirit and the incredible willpower within him.

When I said his name? Well, let's just say I butchered it immediately. As soon as it came out of my mouth, it sounded like an angry sneeze. So, *Ucillino* became Little Bird. Honestly, the name suited him perfectly. From the moment he was carried off that plane, 18 pounds of adorable, raggedy personality in tow, he was my Little Bird. Over time, as my tiny puppy grew into the barrel-chested, 64-pound behemoth of affection he is today, the name Little Bird felt less accurate. Still, it stuck, and now I call him that with a proud kind of defiance, because in my heart, Little Bird is a giant of a dog.

If you think I'm exaggerating about the giant part, let me explain. His upper body is a wrecking ball. His front paws deliver ninja kicks to the back of your knees, and full-on tackles to your shins that'll leave you clutching your legs, as he lands an open-mouthed, slobber-filled love attack, like a slow-motion car crash of affection. He's not gently trying to kiss your face—no, Bird wants to envelop you in his jaws, a canine-tooth excavation, straight up your nostrils!

And don't even get me started on his eye contact. It's like he's staring right through me, locking onto my soul with so much intensity, it feels like he's reading every thought. It's as if he's silently whispering, "I love you so much that I'm going to invade your personal space and leave you wondering if you even remember a time when you could use the bathroom in peace."

But the best part? Bird never apologizes for this. Never. It's as if he's thinking, *Look, I've got one job here on Earth, and that's to love you with everything I've got—all my power, all my little broken bits, my whole messy, wonderful soul. Deal with it.*

And I do. I deal with it every single day, because let's be honest: How could I not love a dog who *owns* his flaws with such ridiculous confidence?

Bird is unlike any dog I've ever known. He doesn't know that he's broken. He's blissfully unaware of his physical limitations. He doesn't care that his legs don't work or that he needs human intervention to pee. He's happy, he's playful, and most importantly, he's tenacious. This big little guy zooms around in his drag bag (yes, drag bag—imagine a potato sack with suspenders) with his muscular front legs propelling him forward while his back legs hang limply behind him. Despite it all, he plays hard. He runs, in his own unique, no-legs-to-hold-him-back kind of way. He lives his life with the kind of pure, untamed joy most of us can only dream of having.

There are also the little moments with Bird that remind me to never take life too seriously. Like the time he ate a dead worm in the yard—because why not? Apparently, worms are delicacies for him, even though both me and my hubby knew he'd puke it up two hours later. But he was in the moment. He didn't care. He was just living, fully and without hesitation.

And then there's Gypsy, one of my other rescue dogs, who came into our lives with a past almost as rough as Bird's. She was hit by a car and left to die in the streets, but when she met Bird, something clicked. It didn't take long for those two damaged souls to form an unbreakable bond. Gypsy, who was once a beaten down, terrified dog, found comfort in Bird. In return, he relied on her for companionship. They became inseparable. It's a beautiful thing to watch, the way they lean on each other, proving that even in the darkest times, love and trust can be found in the most unlikely places.

I should mention that as I'm writing this, Bird is about to go into the hospital for three to five days. I never imagined we'd be here, but here we are. His body, once so determined, is starting to struggle. Bird can't even pee on his own anymore. I've gone back to catheterizing him three times a day, holding my breath every time, hoping I don't accidentally give him another UTI. I fight a daily battle for his health now, and the clock is ticking. Every infection is another reminder that time is running out.

Someday, the vet will tell me the medications no longer work and there's nothing more to do. That day is one I can't even bear to think about. The thought of it twists something deep inside me, like I might lose myself in the emptiness that's bound to follow. Bird is so much more than a dog to me. He's everything.

But even if I feel like I might crumble, I'll have to keep going, if only to honor his existence and save more dogs in his name. And I will. So far, this mess of a journey is teaching me the world's most valuable lesson: I matter. I can impact this world in positive ways, one action at a time, all while healing myself bit by bit.

I know what some of you might be thinking. "It's just a dog," right? But Bird is my constant. He's the one who's been there through some of the hardest times of my life. He's sat by my side through the pain of multiple injuries, surgeries, and the endless uncertainty of undiagnosed illness. He gives me a reason to wake up in the morning, when everything else is falling apart. He's the reason I still believe in unconditional love, in joy, and in life's absurd beauty—even when those things feel like it's slipping away, especially in those dark times when my body seems to betray me. If Bird can do it, then fucking hell, I can too. "Suck it up, Pity Party Barbie!"

I've had other dogs before, dogs that I loved with all my heart, like Ripley, my soul dog who helped me heal, back when my battle with chronic autoimmune illness started. Ripley taught me about resilience, about fighting pain with grace. I lost her to cancer and I will never get over it. There was Boozie, who fought cancer with every ounce of strength she had, but in the end, the disease took her, too. And then, Bird showed up, scrappy and broken but still deserving love, and I knew we had to fight together.

Bird became my reason to keep going. His battle is my battle, his joy is my joy. When I see him running through the yard, dragging his legs behind him in his ridiculously stylish drag bag, that is the exact moment I remember why I'm doing this. It's because life is too short to give up, too short to let the broken parts define us. Bird taught me that. So, I try my hardest to be like Bird.

I know this might all sound dramatic, but let me explain something. I'm not a parent. I've never had kids. I don't know what it's like to lose a child. But the thought of losing Bird someday? That's the closest I'll ever come. The bond we share is deeper than words. And here's the other thing: I get it now. I get what it means to be fully, absolutely depended on by another living creature, to be the one person someone else needs to survive. And it's humbling, terrifying, and beautiful. It's the kind of love that transcends everything. It's the kind of love that gives me a reason to try my hardest. Bird teaches me patience and gratitude. He shows me how to give myself without expecting anything in return. Bird makes me a better human.

So when I wake up every morning to Bird pulling the blankets off, demanding his morning snuggles, I don't care if I'm tired. I don't care if I'm broken. When he lays his body on the floor next to me, paws waving, ready for a belly rub, I remember that life—his life—is a gift. His joy, his love, his unwavering spirit, they're my reminder to take it all in. To chase the butterflies and bark at the ducks. To be absolutely alive.

Watching him thrive has been one of the most humbling and rewarding experiences of my life. It's almost like he was sent to teach me about life, survival, and finding joy in absurdity, even when everything feels impossible. And boy, does he teach.

Here are the lessons Bird has imparted to me about what it means to truly live and love:

1. Nothing is too broken to save: When Bird first came into my life, he was a mess. His back legs were completely useless. His body was frail, almost fragile. His needs? Overwhelming. The people around me said, "You're crazy. He's suffering. It's cruel to keep him alive."

But here's the thing—Bird wasn't suffering. He was *living*. He didn't know his legs were useless. He didn't care that he had to drag his whole body behind him. He was too busy caring about squeaky toys, belly rubs, and chasing the other dogs around the house (mostly for the sole purpose of stealing their toys). He'd sunbathe with his nose high in the air, sniffing at the world like he had all the time in the universe. Watching him, I realized something powerful. No matter how broken something or someone might seem, there's always room for life, love, and happiness to bloom. Bird's survival isn't just a testament to his resilience; it's proof that giving up should never, ever be the first option.

2. Don't let trauma define you: Bird doesn't spend his days mourning the legs he doesn't have or the life he could have lived. Let's be real—he's a dog. Dogs don't sit around contemplating the meaning of existence while pondering whether to bury the bone or chew on it. That's our job as humans. (Maybe just some of us). Bird lives in the now. He squeaks his toys with unbridled enthusiasm. He greets every human like they're his new best friend, because they are. He struts around in his drag bag like he owns the world. For Bird, every day is an adventure. Every human is just one belly rub away from being his bestie.

The way Bird walks through the world is something to aspire to. If I can channel just one ounce of the joi-de-vivre that Bird swears by, I'll be the best version of myself by a mile.

When people ask how I could "be so cruel" to keep him alive, I always smile. Because when they meet Bird, they get it. He's not a tragic story. He's not a sad case. He's a happy, goofy, playful dog who lives life on his own terms. Bird reminds me that no matter what life throws at us, no matter the trauma, we don't have to be defined by our past. We can still live, even with our scars.

3. Poop on the floor, demand belly rubs, don't apologize: Bird is unapologetically himself. If he wants attention, he doesn't ask. He demands it.

Sometimes, that means he waddles across the floor with a squeaky toy in his mouth, leaving a trail of poop behind him (Yep, it's as glamorous as it sounds).

Let's talk about his main method of communication. He doesn't bark like a normal dog–Oh no, that's much too pedestrian. Instead, he lets out this low, rumbling "arggh" noise that sounds like a drunken pirate searching for his missing rum. If the "arggh" doesn't work? He'll escalate to a "grrr" that sounds less threatening and more like he's about to start a mutiny for the sake of belly rubs. If Bird had an eye patch and a little hat, he'd be the canine version of Captain Jack Sparrow—chaos, charm, and a lot of attitude.

Bird doesn't care about his messes. He doesn't apologize for making them. He knows he's loved, with all his imperfections. And that's a lesson we all need to learn. Be like Bird. Don't apologize for your faults or your complications. You deserve love, just as you are.

4. Be clear about your needs: Bird doesn't beat around the bush when it comes to getting what he wants. If he's hungry, he opens a cabinet door with his nose and shoves his head inside. If he needs attention, he doesn't wait for you to make a polite offer. He'll walk up to you and just plow into the back of your knee like a furry bulldozer. If

his drag bag needs adjusting? He'll wiggle and whine until I fix it, or—more likely—until I smell it, myself. It's not good, people. It's like a biologically-engineered time bomb that can go off at any moment.

Bird has taught me to be clear about my needs. This is something I'm still working on. My history has taught me that being too complicated or asking for help can lead to abandonment, but Bird lets me know that it's okay to ask for what you need. The world is full of assholes, so don't waste your time with them. Find someone who values you for vocalizing your needs, someone who's willing to give as much as you're willing to give.

5. Allow people to help you: Bird didn't choose to need me for the basic tasks of life. As much as he may not enjoy certain necessities, like catheterizations or drag bag adjustments, he's learned to accept help. We've developed a routine, a weirdly intimate dance of care, trust, and love.

As someone fiercely independent, Bird's ability to accept help has been a humbling lesson for me. It's not a weakness to lean on others; it's a strength. Bird taught me that allowing people to help you doesn't make you less of a person, it just means you're human.

This isn't just a story about a dog. This is about life. It's a story about choosing to live fully, to love without hesitation, to keep going even when you're broken. It's about finding strength in struggle, finding joy in the mess, and finding love where it's least expected.

The next time life knocks you down, Be Like Bird. Drag yourself forward, demand belly rubs, and never let anyone tell you that you're too broken to keep going. Bird may not have all the answers, but he sure as hell knows how to make the most of every moment. Be like Bird. Live your life, broken and beautiful.

And if you happen to see a brindle, big-headed dog wearing a potato sack and a T-shirt that says "Skipped Leg Day," don't judge me. That shit is hilarious.

LIGHT-IT-UP BARBIE: FINDING & FUELING YOUR PASSION

Do What You Love, Love What You Do

My passion has always been animals, and it's a passion I come by honestly. My mom collected strays the way other moms collected Beanie Babies, and my dad—God bless that man—just learned to roll with it. We rescued the bruised and the broken, literally. Once, my mom brought home a bird with a broken neck from the vet, and somehow, that little bastard lived. From a young age, I learned to love and care for the wounded, the weird, and the hopeless. Turns out, that training would come in handy for adulthood.

There are plenty of things in my life I've forgotten—faces, addresses, entire chapters—but never the animals. Those memories are permanent, tattooed somewhere deep in my heart. I barely remember living in India, but I remember my first cat, Brute: a giant ginger fluff who would tear a bitch up, except for me. I remember my first German Shepherd, Max, loyal and patient in a way most people never were.

I'll never forget my first bird that was truly mine—a crow that flew into our window in Zimbabwe and broke his wing. We helped him heal, expecting he'd take off the second he could. But he didn't. He stayed in our sprawling yard like a little black ghost, following me everywhere, cawing his opinions, and stealing shiny things just to make me chase him. He was my connection to the wild, proof that sometimes love doesn't need a leash or a cage. Later came Cheeky Blue Eye, my first official pet bird, but that crow was the one who taught me what loyalty—and freedom—really looked like.

My animals were my outlet, my forever friends. I wasn't the most outgoing kid; being the blonde girl in countries where that wasn't the norm made me feel like a walking caution sign. I was always kind of an outcast. Case in point: In sixth grade I was voted "Most Unique," which is basically middle-school code for "We can't categorize your weird ass, but we know you don't belong."

When I was growing up, people let me down. Animals never did. They didn't lie, cheat, or gaslight. They just loved. If I had to pick a Disney princess to relate to, it'd be Snow White, but swap the forest for Africa and picture me frolicking with neon-green parakeets instead of deer. I've always understood animals and they've always understood me.

In my early twenties, I started working at Big Cat Rescue—yes, *that* Big Cat Rescue—long before the Tiger King circus came to town. Working with exotic wildlife came naturally to me. I loved it. The adrenaline, the purpose, the sense that I was doing something bigger than myself, it all lit me up from the inside. But life has a way of dimming even the brightest lights. As the years rolled on and the wrong men rolled in, I started losing pieces of myself. Abusive relationships have a way of convincing you that your light is inconvenient. I traded the roar of lions for the silence of survival, and for a while, I forgot who I was.

Then came Ripley, my soul dog. When she died, the grief cracked me open, but it also pushed me forward. The day after she passed, I called a local rescue and asked how I could help. I started small—cleaning cages, showing up at events—but each act felt like breathing again. Volunteering became my therapy.

That rescue, though, was a disaster. The owner wasn't actually taking care of the dogs, and it broke my heart. Now, let me be very clear—this isn't a rescue-bashing session. No one gets into animal rescue for fame or fortune. They start with good intentions and open hearts. But I've seen it firsthand: The burnout, the heartbreak, the quiet devastation that creeps in when you realize that no matter how many dogs you save, it will never be enough.

Here's the brutal truth that sits in your soul once you've seen too much: Until humanity catches up and realizes we aren't the only fucking life on this planet that matters, dogs, cats, and every other creature will keep paying the price for our narcissism.

Okay. Rant over. Let's continue.

Where other people saw hopelessness, I saw a challenge. I started coordinating with other rescues, finding fosters, and rehoming dogs one by one. Every adoption felt like a small miracle. I learned that heartbreak is also a spark. The worse that situation got, the more determined I became. I couldn't fix everything, but I could fix something.

I refused to let those dogs go down with the ship. I made calls. I begged for fosters. I reached out to other rescues, coordinated transport, and made sure every single one of those dogs had a chance. And in the middle of all that chaos, somewhere between the exhaustion and the hope, I realized something huge: This wasn't just about saving dogs anymore.

It was about saving myself.

Every adoption, every reunion, every wagging tail felt like a tiny piece of my own healing slipping back into place. The work was messy and thankless and sometimes impossible, but it gave me purpose again. The more I poured into rescue, the more I came alive. That's the thing about passion—it demands your whole heart, but it makes your heart beat even stronger.

Soon, weekends at adoption events weren't enough. I wanted to do more, to make the system better instead of just mopping up its mess. I joined a board and took on more fosters. Before I knew it, I was waist-deep in spreadsheets, vet bills, and event plans—and I loved every second of it. I wasn't just volunteering anymore; I was rebuilding.

When I say "events," I don't mean bake-sale bullshit with stale brownies and folding tables. I mean full-on productions—charity galas, casino nights, costume parties, and silent auctions that brought in thousands for the dogs. I used every ounce of creativity, every connection, every scrap of marketing magic I'd honed in my career, and funneled it straight into rescue. I built campaigns, crafted partnerships, and convinced people that giving a damn was sexy again.

Somewhere in that whirlwind of chaos, dogs, and glitter, something beautiful happened. I stopped surviving and started thriving. I was no longer just someone who'd been hurt, someone who was trying to heal. I was a woman on fire, turning purpose into movement.

Rescue became my rebellion, my revolution against apathy and cruelty, against my own past. Every dog I helped find a home felt like reclaiming another piece of my voice. I was doing something that mattered, not for recognition, but for redemption.

That's when I realized what purpose really is. It's not some grand cosmic assignment written in the stars. It's what happens when passion collides with compassion and refuses to die out.

That's where Light-It-Up Barbie was born, the Barbie who doesn't wait for inspiration to strike. She builds it, brick by brick, heartbreak by heartbreak. She's the spark that refuses to stay small.

Light-It-Up Barbie Lights the Way

There's a saying that captures the heart of rescue work: "You can't change the world for all dogs, but you can change the world for one."

If any of my alter egos embodies that statement, it's Light-It-Up Barbie. She's got a full heart, a clear mission, and an unrelenting sense of purpose. She's the glimmer in the dark, the flash in the storm, the voice that whispers, *keep going, there's still good left to do.*

When life knocks me down—and it does—Light-It-Up Barbie is the one who grabs me by the metaphorical ponytail and drags me out of bed. She reminds me that somewhere out there, a dog is waiting for someone like me to show up. And if I can do that—if I can help one more—then I've done enough for today.

She reminds me that I matter, because the way I exist in the world matters. I still get texts from families who adopted dogs I fostered—holiday photos, stories, updates. I didn't just save a dog; I helped build a family. I connected a broken animal to a healing human, and together they created something beautiful. That's what purpose looks like. It's a ripple that turns into a wave.

No matter who you are or what your passion is, you have the power to change someone's life, even if you never see the outcome. That's the magic of living with purpose. You may never see how far your light travels, but trust me, it travels.

That's what gets me up in the morning, even on days when my body's screaming *stay down.* There's always another dog that needs help, another lonely person waiting to find their fur-soulmate, another spark waiting to be lit. That's the beauty of passion: It turns heartbreak into horsepower.

Action #5: Find Your Passion

Here's my advice: Stop waiting for passion to tap you on the shoulder like some divine epiphany. Passion doesn't whisper, it grabs you by the throat and commands you to move. You have to make your own meaning, which involves finding the one thing that lets you go to bed at night and say, "Everything is on fire, but at least today, I mattered."

If that thing makes you feel a little crazy, or obsessive, or overly invested? Good. That's called caring. Finding your passion isn't about proving something to the world. It's about proving something to yourself. What makes you feel alive? What makes the noise stop? What makes the hard days worth it? That's your thing.

When I started posting about my rescue work, someone I knew tried to knock me down a peg. They commented, "You do all this shit for dogs that doesn't mean a damn thing, but you don't care about starving children or homeless people."

Cool story, Karen. At least I'm doing something.

That's the thing about passion—it terrifies people who don't have their own. When someone tries to make you feel small for caring, it's usually because your light makes them realize how dim theirs has gotten. Don't dim yourself for anyone. Don't apologize for your fire. Don't shrink to make someone else comfortable. You're here to light it up.

Find one thing to care about and start there. Feed someone. Foster something. Make one donation. Volunteer once. The world doesn't need you to fix it all. It just needs you to give a damn about one corner of it. If even half of the planet did one small, kind, purposeful thing, the ripple effect would change everything. Passion doesn't have to be grand or glamorous. It just has to move you.

Your passion might be art, poetry, animals, teaching, cooking, spreadsheets, or succulents. Whatever it is, chase it. Obsess over it. Nurture it. Let it remind you that you're alive. Take my friend Jackson, for example. His wife is an artist, he's not. But the man can cook. I'm talking Cajun magic, the kind of food that makes you weep over the gumbo pot. I told him, "Jackson, your passion isn't painting. It's feeding people. That's your art."

He's fed half his neighborhood, mentored young chefs, helped people open restaurants, all because he followed his joy. That's what passion does. It multiplies. It's contagious in the best possible way.

Most people *do* know what their passion is, they're just too close to see it—forest for the trees and all that. So, ask the people who love you: *What am I good at? What do you see in me that I don't see in myself?* Sometimes your spark is hiding behind your own self-doubt.

If you're scared to follow your passion at

first, that's fine. Start small. Don't sign up to chair a board on day one. Walk one dog. Paint one canvas. Write one paragraph. Grow one plant that doesn't die immediately. A cactus counts. Yes, it's a low bar, but still, it's progress.

Passion isn't about perfection. It's about participation. It's about showing up, even when you're tired, even when you're scared, even when it feels pointless. When I'm knee-deep in rescue work, exhausted and overwhelmed, I remind myself that I'm not doing this to be perfect. I'm doing this to matter.

That's the real secret.

At the end of the day, what lets you go to bed and say, "Everything might be shit, but I mattered today"? No one else needs to believe it. You just need to know it's true. Maybe your passion is writing. Don't aim for a novel, just write a sentence. Write a haiku. Hell, write a grocery list if it feels good.

Maybe you love plants but kill everything you touch. Start with a succulent. Name it something sturdy, like Gary the Survivor. The point isn't to be perfect. The point is to participate in your own joy.

If you don't know what your passion is, go find it. Try everything. Try the things you used to love before life broke your heart. Go back to the last time you were happy. Maybe it was fingerpainting in fifth grade. Perfect. Start fingerpainting again. You don't need to be Picasso. You just need to remember what joy feels like.

Let me tell you about a woman I met at the vet once. Her dog had just died and a year before that, her husband died. She told me she'd spent her whole life doing everything he loved. After he died, she didn't know who she was anymore.

She started over. She moved into an assisted-living community and said yes to everything. Shuffleboard. Pilates. Water aerobics. (She hated them all.) But eventually, she found things that stuck: Reading, a book club, and another dog. She opened her heart again, and that changed everything.

That's what I mean when I say light it up. Even in the ashes of loss, you can find a spark.

So, be like that woman. Try everything. Restart. Reignite. Because life isn't about finding the perfect passion, it's about remembering that you're still capable of feeling alive.

Self-Reflection: Light Your Own Fire

Before you close this chapter, take a minute to turn the mirror on yourself. Don't be scared. Just be honest.

1. When was the last time you tried something new, even when you weren't sure if you'd be good at it?
2. What's something you used to love doing but somehow left behind? What would it feel like to start again?
3. Think of a time you failed but learned something about who you are. Would you take that risk again, knowing what you know now?
4. When you picture your happiest moments, what are you doing? Who's with you? What does that say about what truly lights you up?
5. If you stripped away everyone else's expectations—your family's, your boss's, your partner's—what's left? What would you choose to pour your time, love, and energy into?

6. What kind of impact do you want to leave, even if no one ever knows it was you?

Take your time with these questions. Sit in them. Scribble your answers in the margins. Think them over in the shower. The goal isn't to figure it all out tonight. It's to start a conversation with yourself that will guide you to becoming the truest version of yourself.

Here's the hard but beautiful truth: Your passion isn't out there, waiting somewhere you can't reach. It's been inside you all along, waiting for you to light it up.

BADASS BARBIE GETS IT DONE

Get Up, Show Up, Fuck Shit Up

Here's the thing nobody tells you when you're sitting in the smoking rubble of your life, wondering what the actual fuck happened: no one is coming to save you. There is no cavalry charging over the hill, no fairy godmother with a glittery wand, no cosmic alignment waiting to hand you a do-over. You've got two choices—move or die. And dying doesn't always mean a body in the ground. Sometimes it's the slow, soul-rotting kind. The kind where you stay too long in the wrong job, the wrong relationship, the wrong version of yourself, until you're nothing more than a half-alive ghost with Wi-Fi and a decent skincare routine.

I wish I could tell you I figured that out gracefully, sipping green juice in my power leggings while journaling about "alignment." Nope. I learned it the hard way, with my back against the wall, the clock ticking, and fear screaming in my face like it paid rent. But I stopped asking that bitch for permission. I didn't have a plan. I didn't have a roadmap. I had a fucking pulse. And a pulse is enough to start.

Helpful hint: When you finally decide to move, the universe won't high-five you. It'll test you. It'll throw boulders in your path and whisper, *Let's see how bad you really want this*. People will doubt you. Others will vanish—poof—taking their fake-ass support with them. But the real war? It's not against them. It's against the version of you that keeps whispering, *Maybe later*. The you that crawls back to comfort every damn time. The you that confuses waiting with preparing.

Motion doesn't require readiness. It just requires one shaky step and the stubborn refusal to stay where you are. That's how Badass Barbie was born—not because I woke up fearless, but because I finally told hesitation to sit the fuck down and shut up.

Badass Barbie Tags In

Badass Barbie wasn't some shiny new persona or a makeover moment where I woke up fearless and fabulous. She'd been there all along, battle-tested, scarred up, and patiently waiting for me to stop playing small. She's the grit that got me through every storm, the defiant voice whispering, "Get the fuck up." I didn't invent her, I just finally stopped muting her.

I learned that the hard way, the day I realized I was living like my demons were still in the room. I was still armored up, still swinging at shadows, still lashing out at people who hadn't done a damn thing to deserve it. My fuse was short, my defenses were sharp, and I was surviving battles that didn't exist anymore. When you've lived in constant defense mode, cruelty becomes second nature. You learn to cut first, feel later. It's not weakness or cruelty, it's survival. But the thing no one tells you? Survival doesn't know when to stop.

For years, I wore my anger like a designer jacket—tailored, familiar, and heavy as hell. I told myself I had the right to it. I didn't get the "Donna Reed" life. I didn't have a mother who tucked me in and told me everything would be okay. I clung to that bitterness like it was proof that I'd endured something, and maybe it was. But it also kept me chained to the past, staring at everything I didn't have instead of everything I did. While I was keeping score, I ignored the wins: Grandparents who showed up, a roof over my head, opportunities that other people would kill for. Gratitude can't grow in soil soaked with resentment.

That resentment made me hard. It made me careless. Reckless. I'd scorch the earth with my words and call it honesty. I wasn't being real; I was being reactive. My mouth was a loaded gun and I didn't care who I hit, because pain had convinced me I was bulletproof.

The turning point wasn't cinematic. No music swelling in the background, no dramatic epiphany. It was quiet. I'd just unloaded on someone who didn't deserve it. My heart was still racing, adrenaline humming, when I looked up and saw their face. Not angry. Not scared. Just hurt. That look wrecked me. Because it was the same look I used to have when *he* tore me down. And that's when I knew that I'd become the thing I swore I'd never be.

That realization gutted me. I thought I was fighting not to be a victim. But somewhere along the way, I'd started fighting everyone. So, I did the thing I used to mock: I got help. Counseling. Anger management. Not for a gold star or a sob story, but because if I didn't, I was going to keep bleeding on people who didn't cut me.

I learned to press pause. To wait before reacting. To breathe before detonating. I created rules for myself: Never send the email in the moment. Write it. Wait 24 hours. If it still felt right the next day, hit send. (Spoiler: It usually didn't.)

I didn't come out the other side enlightened and glowing. I'm still a work in messy, magnificent progress. I still have a tongue that could slice through steel and a temper that could fuel a small country. But now, I know when to pull back. I know that power without control is just chaos in heels.

Here's the thing nobody celebrates: Taking responsibility for your own bullshit hurts. There's no applause for realizing you're the problem. No trophy for saying, "I fucked this up." But that's the real work. That's where growth lives, in the quiet moments when you stop pointing fingers and start looking in the mirror.

Badass Barbie didn't arrive, she got tagged back in. She's been fighting alongside me my whole life. Through every heartbreak, every trauma, every "move or die" moment where I clawed my way forward. I just forgot she was there. She's the part of me that knows when to stand up, when to shut up, and when to burn the whole thing down and rebuild.

Badass Barbie isn't fearless, she's just done being controlled by fear. She walks into the fire when it's worth it and walks away when it's not. She doesn't need permission, validation, or a fucking audience. She moves with purpose, grit, and heart.

So no, this wasn't the day Badass Barbie was born. It was the day I finally stopped benching her. The day I remembered who the hell I was. Once she stepped back into the light, heels clicking and eyes blazing, I knew one thing for sure: There was no fucking going back.

The Badass Barbie Archetype

Badass Barbie isn't just a plastic doll, wrapped in cellophane, sitting quietly on a shelf. She's not perfect, but she's also not pretending to be, and she sure as hell isn't here to please everyone. She's the version of you that finally steps into the room like she belongs there—because she sure as fuck does.

She's born the moment you stop outsourcing your power. She shows up when you quit waiting for someone to apologize, to notice you, or to hand you permission. Badass Barbie writes her own permission slip. And yeah, she's unapologetic about it, because she's not running on ego, she's running on clarity.

She knows her worth. She's done the work to figure out who she is and what she brings to the table and she doesn't discount herself for anyone. She sets hard boundaries, not as walls to hide behind, but as lines in the sand that keep her aligned with her goals.

She's strategic with her hell-fire. She can still throw down when she must, but she's learned that restraint is its own kind of power. She commands her space, whether she's in a boardroom, at a job site, or sitting around a kitchen table with her closest friends. She doesn't shrink to make anyone else comfortable, she expands and invites them to rise with her.

Badass Barbie moves with intention. No more knee-jerk reactions that torch bridges. Every move is deliberate, not from fear, but from experience. She knows that real power lives in the pause. Becoming Badass Barbie isn't about getting louder. It's about getting sharper while still letting your compassion come through. It's about moving from a reactive place to an intentional presence.

From "I hope they like me" to "I know my value." From proving you're worthy to protecting your peace.

Badass Barbie asks herself questions before she speaks or acts: Is this worth my time and energy? Does this move me forward? Will this matter in a year? If it's a no, she lets that shit go. If it's a yes, she goes all in—heart, heels, and hustle. She's not afraid to walk away from toxic people, half-baked opportunities, or old stories that keep her small, the ones steeped in fear, the ones that don't allow her to bloom.

The world doesn't reward women who wait their turn. It rewards the ones who are ready when the moment comes, the ones who've done the work, owned their past, and sharpened their edge without losing their heart or humanity. That's what makes Badass Barbie different from the "Boss Babe" fluff you see on Instagram. She's not a hashtag. She's a woman who has earned her seat at the table. And she's not here to play small.

When Badass Barbie Gets to Work

There was this one work project I'll never forget, the kind where everyone's running around like overly caffeinated squirrels, pointing fingers, and pretending that "waiting on feedback" is a legitimate strategy. The deadline had been moved so many times it should have had its own forwarding address. Every delay cost us time, money, and the will to live. The fact that I didn't stab myself in the eye with a dull spoon is a miracle.

Old me would've gone full chaos commander—barking orders, sending aggressive, all-caps emails, and mainlining coffee like a coping mechanism. I would have tried to hold the entire thing together with spreadsheets, stress, and a bag full of F-bombs. But Badass Barbie doesn't run on panic anymore. She runs on precision, purpose, and yes, caffeine. But mostly purpose.

Instead of joining the meltdown parade, I got the facts. I walked in with a plan tighter than my jeans after Thanksgiving: Clear deadlines, named owners, and zero wiggle room for excuses. I didn't sugarcoat it, but I also didn't waste time assigning blame. Blame doesn't fix broken workflows, it just makes the meetings longer.

Of course, there was pushback. There always is. Some people act like accountability is a hate crime. One guy told me I was being "too direct," which is corporate for "you made me uncomfortable by being competent." That's fine. I wasn't there to win Miss Congeniality, I was there to stop the train from derailing.

Then, something shifted. The doers started doing. The talkers got quiet. The professional excuse-makers suddenly discovered "other projects." By the end of the week, we hit the deadline. The same people who side-eyed me on Monday were thanking me by Friday, like I'd performed a small-scale corporate exorcism.

Badass Barbie isn't the loudest in the room, she's the one who walks in with a plan, a pulse, and a purpose. She doesn't need applause, she needs alignment. The win isn't the praise, it's that quiet, almost smug satisfaction of watching chaos finally obey.

True leadership isn't about being liked. It's about keeping your cool while everything burns, handing out marching orders with a smile, and walking out of the dumpster fire holding a color-coded binder, announcing, "Well, that was productive."

Reader Application: How to Act When You're Stuck

You might not want to hear this, but I say it with a big dose of tough love: Nobody's coming to rescue you. If you're sitting around waiting for the perfect time, the perfect plan, or the perfect version of yourself, grab a snack, because you'll be waiting forever.

No one owes you anything. You owe yourself everything. You owe yourself the attempt. The forward motion. The fight. Because if you don't move, you don't grow, and staying stuck too long is just another way of dying slowly.

You can't expect a rainbow at the end of every storm. Life isn't a highlight reel. It's raw, unpredictable, and often unfair. Sometimes it's breathtaking, but mostly, it's work. Life isn't about the things that happen to you, it's about what you do with those things. I gave up once in my life—technically three times—and I'll never do it again. I'm here to stay. That's the Badass Barbie part of me. She doesn't wait for permission or the "right moment." She creates it. And when she feels herself stalling, stalling, she's got a playbook.

Badass Barbie knows big problems aren't walls—they're puzzles. You don't solve them with dramatic sighs. Trust me, I've tried. They don't come down with one swing. You have to go piece by piece. When the goal feels too big, shrink it down. One call. One email. One small, deliberate move forward. Don't waste energy mapping the entire mountain before you've taken the first step.

Badass Barbie also knows that accountability is the secret sauce to life. Find someone who will call you on your bullshit. Not a cheerleader, not a comfort-zone companion. You need the person who will look you dead in the eye and say, "Why isn't this done yet?" Give them permission to be brutally honest, even when it stings. Growth doesn't always feel good, but it does feel worthwhile.

When the going gets tough, Badass Barbie doesn't crumble, she focuses. She sets deadlines that actually matter, because a deadline you blow off isn't a deadline, it's a wish on a Post-it. She doesn't only apply that mindset to work; it's for everything. Cleaning out that closet you've been avoiding? Call it "Operation Emotional Declutter" and give yourself a due date. Booking that doctor's appointment, finishing that half-painted wall, or making a date with your laundry pile? Schedule tasks like they're a board meeting with your future self.

Tie your goals to something real, something that actually matters: Your paycheck, your reputation, your relationships, your pride. Hell, even your sanity. You can't thrive in chaos if you're constantly tripping over your own to-do list. Pressure isn't your enemy, it's your fuel.

Badass Barbie doesn't wait for someone else to set the pace. She doesn't need a boss breathing down her neck. She sets her own expectations and then she outperforms them, preferably with a playlist blasting, paying homage to 90's boy bands. She's the CEO of Getting Shit Done.

Leave the *can'ts* and *won'ts* in the past. Those words don't match your outfit anymore. The pressure you feel? That's not your enemy, it's your edge. It's the spark that reminds you you're capable of more. Diamonds don't form without a little heat and neither does progress.

When life piles on—the bills, the chores, the chaos—don't throw your hands up. Channel your inner Badass Barbie, slap on a power bun, and say, "Fine. Let's do this." Adopt the two-minute rule: If something can be done in two minutes or less, do it now. Respond to the email. Schedule the call. Put the damn appointment in your calendar. Two minutes of action now will save you two hours of mental clutter later. Those quick wins will start stacking up, and before you know it, you've built real momentum.

Here's Badass Barbie's secret: She still gets scared and overwhelmed, but she moves anyway. She takes a deep breath, wipes off yesterday's mascara, and steps forward, even when her brain is screaming, "Are you sure about this?"

She's learned that power doesn't come from being fearless; it comes from showing up scared, tired, maybe still in sweatpants, and doing the thing anyway. You don't need a cape—or clean hair—to be brave. You don't need to feel ready to start. You just need to start. Confidence doesn't lead to action; action creates confidence. Half the courage you're looking for only shows up once you're already in motion.

Here's your challenge: pick one thing you've been avoiding. You know the one—the task that's been staring at you from your to-do list like a judgmental cat. Stop giving it more power than it deserves. Do it today. Before your head hits the pillow tonight, take one real step. Don't overthink it. Just act. Then soak in that weird, electric rush of pride that comes from actually doing the damn thing.

When you're tempted to quit, remember this: Action beats inspiration every single time. You don't need motivation; you need motion.

That's what separates the dreamers from the doers. That's what builds trust in yourself. That's what makes you unstoppable—no heels required.

Action #6: Act and Get Results

There are so many people who sugarcoat things and say that everything will be okay. But it won't always be okay. I think that's the scariest and hardest part of life: If you don't do anything, you stay stuck and probably won't be okay. And if you're not okay, chances are that you're unintentionally pulling down the people around you, too.

Take action because you love the people around you. They think you're worth something, because you are. But if you don't see it in yourself, how can they keep believing it for you? You have to make a choice. All you really have at the end of the day, at the end of the noise and chaos, is you.

You can't outsource your growth. You can't delegate your healing. You have to swim or drown. Whatever version of life you want, you have to build it piece by piece, with your own two hands. And when you do—when you act—you start getting results. You start finding proof that you can trust yourself again, proof that you are capable, that you can still fight for something better. The stars are still within reach, because they were always meant for you.

Decisive action doesn't just change your to-do list, it changes your life. When you stop waiting for perfect conditions and just start moving, the wins pile up faster than you expect. In my world, taking action has played out in three specific ways.

First, there was a job that paid the bills but bled me dry. Every morning felt heavier than the last, and I forgot what it felt like to actually enjoy what I did. Badass Barbie doesn't do slow death by boredom and politics. I didn't wait for a perfect backup plan or a magical safety net. I left. And almost immediately, all the energy I'd wasted staying stuck became fuel to start building something better. It wasn't easy—it was terrifying—but freedom rarely comes wrapped in comfort.

Next, I boldly asked for the job I wanted and got the "yes" I deserved. Opportunity doesn't always knock politely. Sometimes you have to kick down the door and announce yourself. There was a role I knew I could crush, but no one was offering it. I came in with a plan, a point, and proof that I could deliver— No apologies, no pretending to be small. They said yes, not because I was lucky, but because I was ready. It reminded me that asking for what you've earned is its own kind of power.

Finally, I took back my health on my own terms. For years, I told myself I'd focus on my health when life "calmed down," but it never did. So I stopped waiting for permission from my schedule, from people, from chaos. I made the appointments. I changed my habits. I decided I was done living at half capacity. My body still hurts. Some days are harder than I'll ever admit out loud. But I keep moving. I keep showing up. And on the days I can't, I've learned to reach for the people who love me and let them hold me up until I can stand again.

None of these steps were giant leaps. They were choices, moments when I chose action over avoidance, clarity over chaos, myself over other people's comfort. Every time, those choices built a new version of me: Steadier, braver, louder in the right ways.

That's the power of movement. Once you start, the next step comes easier. Then the next. Before you know it, you're not reacting to life anymore, you're directing it.

Questions to Ask Yourself

1. Where in your life are you waiting for permission to change?
2. What have you convinced yourself is fine, but deep down, it's quietly destroying you?
3. What's one thing you could walk away from that would make room for something better?
4. What's one small action that your future self will thank you for taking today?
5. And maybe most importantly, what's the cost of doing nothing?

Your Move

We've covered a lot in this chapter. We started with the gut-punch truth: Waiting for the perfect moment is just another way of giving your power away. We dug into the Badass Barbie archetype, not as some cutesie little label but as a way of moving through life with clarity, precision, and zero apologies for wanting more. We looked at the exact tools that keep you from stalling out, from shrinking problems into doable steps to building real accountability, the kind that keeps you honest. We saw what action-in-motion looks like in real life: Walking away from what drains you and taking back control of your own well-being.

If you've been paying attention, you already know this. Change is never about one massive, cinematic leap. It's about a thousand small, deliberate choices that stack up until one day you look around and realize you're living in a reality you built yourself.

That's exactly why this chapter belongs here, at the end. None of the insight, none of the lessons, and none of the self-awareness you've gained from this book will mean a thing if you stop here.

The temptation will be real. You'll close the book, feel fired up for a day or two, then slip back into old habits. You'll start telling yourself those same soft lies: "I'll do it when things calm down. I'll start after I'm ready. I just need to think about it more."

Badass Barbie doesn't wait. She acts when she's tired. She acts when she's scared. She acts when she doesn't know exactly how it's going to play out. She knows that motion creates momentum, and momentum is what produces results.

Here's the bigger truth. This is no longer about a chapter. This is about the life you want and the person you've decided to be. Every principle you've read in these pages has been about reclaiming your agency, sharpening your decision-making, and building a spine that holds steady under pressure. You've seen what's possible when you stop asking for permission and start owning your choices.

Now comes the part no one can do for you: Living your own life.

You're going to have days when you feel unstoppable and days when you want to hide under the covers. Both are part of the process. The difference between people who build the life they want and those who don't is not talent or luck. It's the willingness to keep showing up when it's inconvenient and uncomfortable, when it feels like no one is noticing.

That's what every win in this chapter, and this book, has in common. It's about the quiet courage to take the step in front of you without knowing exactly where the road ends. It's about choosing action over perfection. It's about refusing to let fear be the loudest voice in the room.

So here's my challenge to you, not just for today but for the rest of your life: Stop waiting for clarity. Stop waiting for confidence. Stop waiting for someone to validate your worth. Decide what you want, take the smallest possible action toward it today, and repeat that every day until it's yours.

No one is coming to do this for you. No one cares about your goals as much as you do. No one will hand you the perfect conditions. If you let that reality depress you instead of fuel you, you've missed the point. This isn't a curse. It's freedom.

It means you are in control. You get to decide. You get to build. You get to change your mind, pivot, and start over as many times as you need to. Every time you choose action over avoidance, you teach yourself that you can be trusted to follow through. You prove that you're not just dreaming about a different life, you're creating it.

When you land on the last page of a book, you have two choices. You can file it away as "something inspiring I read once," or you can treat it as a contract with yourself. If you're still here, reading this, I'm betting you're ready for the second option.

Don't let this be another thing you meant to do something with. Let it be the turning point. Let it be the line in the sand where you stopped being a passenger in your own story and started being the driver. There's no choice but to keep moving forward, and that's coming from someone who tried to end her own life.

Close the gap between who you are now and who you want to be, not with one giant leap, but with the relentless, unglamorous discipline of showing up. Let every decision, every conversation, and every risk you take reinforce the truth that you are capable, resourceful, and done playing small.

The final takeaway is simple: Start now. Start messy. Start scared. Don't wait for someone else to give you permission. Don't wait until things are perfect. Just start. And keep going until the life you are living looks like the one you've been fighting for. Because you are the only one who can make that happen. And you are absolutely capable of doing it. Close this book and go. You already have everything you need. Now prove it to yourself.

If you're still reading this, it means you made it through my story—through the glitter bombs and the battle cries, the dark nights, the WTFs, and the deeply weird Barbie metaphors—and damn, you're my kind of human. Thank you for hanging in there. For walking with me through the chaos, the healing, the honesty, and the hilarity.

Life's not a clean arc or a neat little story—it's a choose-your-own-adventure where half of the map is on fire, you're in heels you forgot you packed, and somehow, you're still standing. Still curious. Still here.

So, what now? Oh, just changing my entire life. Again. And maybe writing a fucking book today. Or maybe *you* will. Whatever comes next, I hope it's messy and magical and unapologetically yours. Because the next chapter? It's already waiting. And you, you gorgeous manifestation of glitter and stardust, you are more than ready.

Acknowledgements

ACKNOWLEDGEMENTS

To the ones who stayed when they didn’t have to: You didn't just stick by me, you gorilla-glued your hearts to mine, even when I was more chaos-gremlin than functioning human. Thank you for loving me through the meltdowns, the mood swings, the “I'm fine” lies, and the years when I thought a platinum buzz cut was an excellent decision. You are my chosen family. You stayed with me, even when I tried to push you away. That makes you either saints or lunatics. Probably both and I love you for it.

To my dad: You never gave up on me. Not when I was lost, when I was messy, when I was at my most unlovable. You've believed in every version of me, including the ones I wanted to delete. Your love is a lighthouse. Thank you for always shining, even when I drifted too far.

And to my husband: My everything. My calm in the storm, my partner in crime, my reason to believe in magic and second chances. You've seen me at my absolute worst and you still looked at me like I hung the moon. Loving you is the easiest thing I've ever done. You are the plot twist I didn't see coming, the one that made the whole story make sense. If people aren't ugly-crying with jealousy right now, they need to reread this paragraph, so they know to never settle for less than they deserve, which is everything.

www.ingramcontent.com/pod-product-compliance
Lightning Source LLC
LaVergne TN
LVHW010714061126
851857LV00014B/1177
9798997767808